W9-BGW-951

101 GOLF COURSES

101 GOLF COURSES

A tour of the best and most uplifting golf courses in the world

Geoffrey Giles

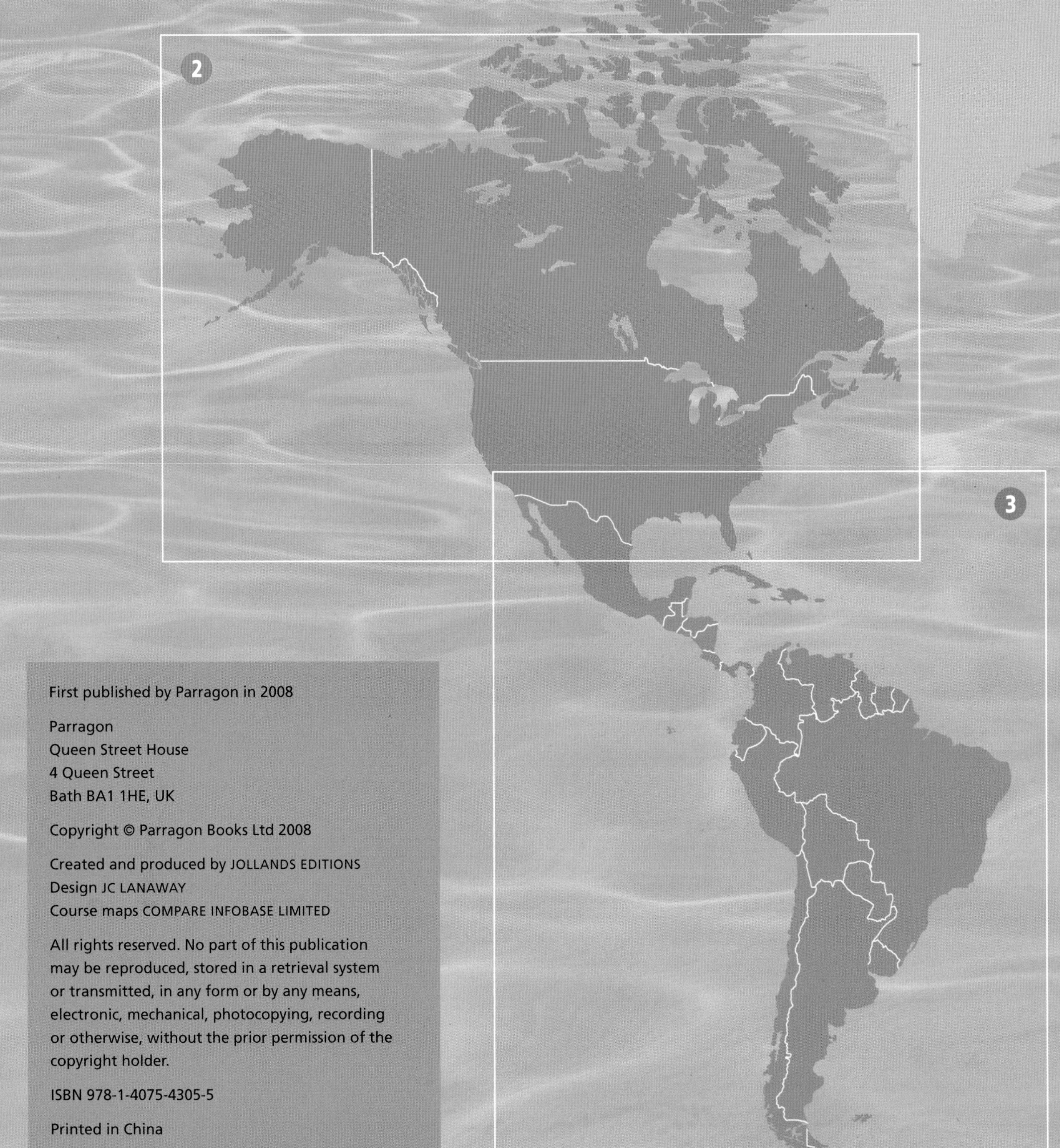

First published by Parragon in 2008

Parragon
Queen Street House
4 Queen Street
Bath BA1 1HE, UK

Created and produced by JOLLANDS EDITIONS
Design JC LANAWAY
Course maps COMPARE INFOBASE LIMITED

ISBN 978-1-4075-4305-5

Printed in China

PRACTICAL DETAILS

Most of the courses in this book welcome visiting golfers, the exceptions being some private clubs, mainly in the United States and Canada. The famous championship courses are inundated with requests to play, so book well in advance. Club websites will usually include details of fees, availability, handicap restrictions, dress codes, and whether a letter of introduction is required, and many will have an online booking facility.

Distances in the book are given in yards, which are used in North America and—still, despite metrication—by the golfing community in Great Britain.

Scorecards give the hole lengths from the back or championship tees as they were at the time of writing. Note that, for championships, what might be a short par 5 for the members is sometimes re-designated as a long par 4 for competitors. Clubs frequently build new tees or simply remeasure their course, so these distances should only be used as a guideline.

Every effort has been made to check facts thoroughly, but errors may have crept in. The publisher would be grateful for corrections or information helpful for future editions.

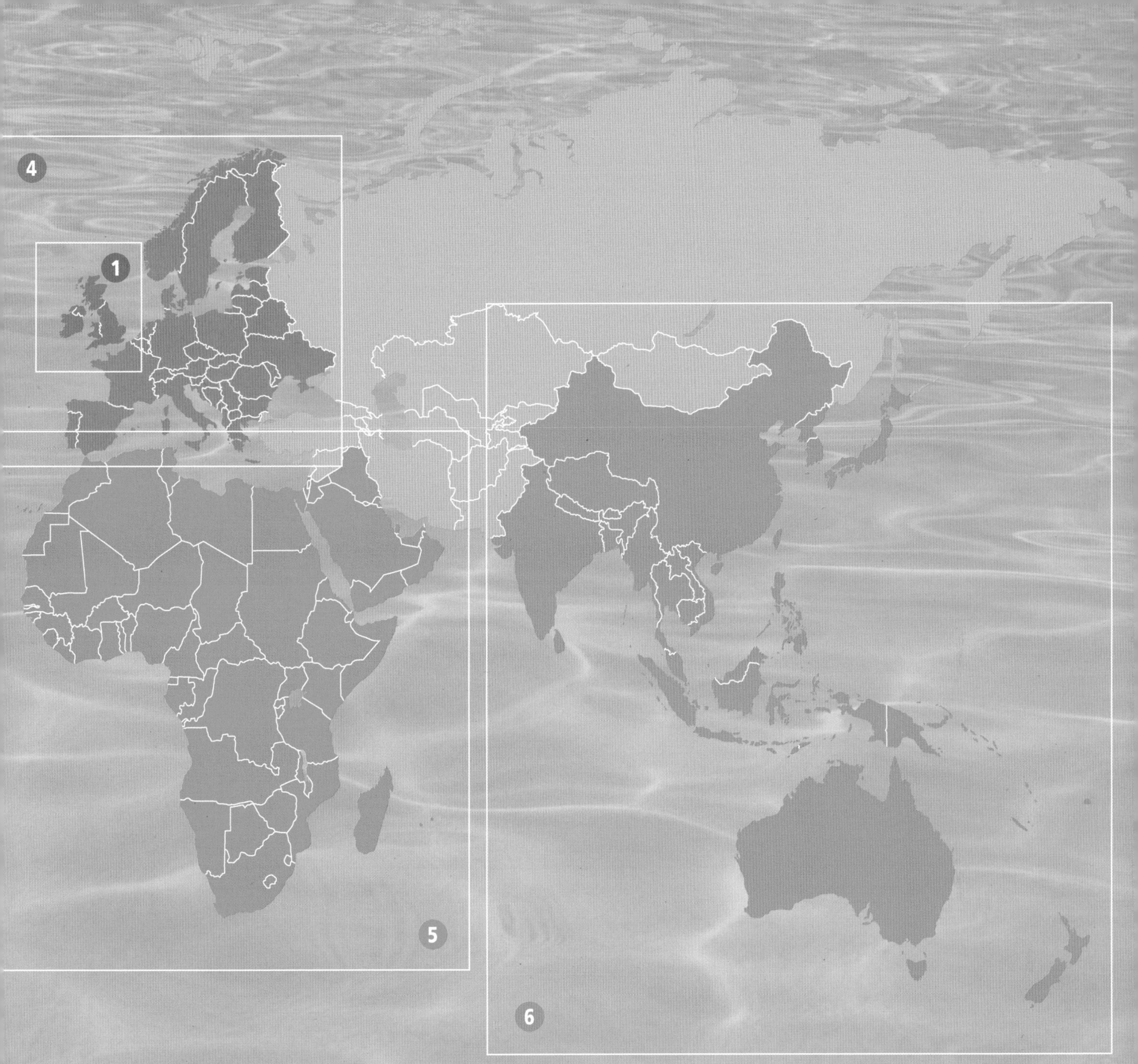

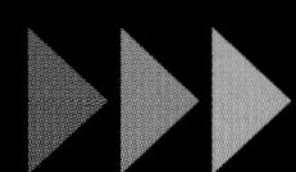

Contents

Introduction

It was the great English-born American golf course designer Robert Trent Jones who wrote, "The first golf course architect, of course, was the Lord, and he was the best there has ever been." The early golfers of Scotland and the Netherlands played their golf on relatively undefined patches of ground wherever they happened to live. There was no such thing as a typical golf course. And while a few elements of a course have become standardized, there is still no standard golf course.

The Scots became the defining influence on golf when the Honourable Company of Edinburgh Golfers laid down the first set of rules in 1744. In 1754 twenty-two "Noblemen and Gentlemen" gathered in St. Andrews to form the Royal and Ancient Golf Club of St. Andrews (R&A), and the newcomers gradually gained the ascendancy. Their rules dealt mainly with the situations that might occur during the course of a match—the rules of matchplay. You played against each other, not against the course. Medal play would have been unthinkable, because the number of holes per course varied until St. Andrews, which had now reduced its course to one of 18 holes, standardized this number for a round of golf in 1858.

ABOVE *The spiritual home of golf, St. Andrews. The R&A does not own the golf courses—the Old Course is one of several run by the Links Management Trust on behalf of the town. Visitors may book online, by post, or by telephone far in advance, take advantage of one of the golf tour operators' packages, or take pot luck in one of the daily ballots.*

BELOW *Royal County Down, originally laid out by Old Tom Morris over 100 years ago.*

In the mid-19th century men began to "design" golf courses. The great players of the day were called upon to lay out the "links" of newly formed golf clubs. Those great players were all Scottish and they all played on the links courses of Scotland, on that strip of unfertile, sandy soil between the beach and the town or farmland. Inevitably they tried to recreate the features that gave their home courses distinction. They looked for green sites in hollows, which would be self-watering with dew, or on humps and hillocks, because they tested technique. Sand exposed by sheep sheltering from the wind or natural erosion had become a common feature of links, and these were replicated by early bunkers.

Today's golf course designers are master craftsmen, and they are doing just what Allan Robertson, Tom Morris and Willie Park did a century and a half ago. They now have the benefit of computer-aided design, sophisticated earthmoving machines, real-estate lawyers, civil engineers, and environmentalists. Given the restraints of what they may be allowed to do, ecologically, and the dire consequences of getting it the tiniest bit wrong, we should rejoice that the greatest players of our day are prepared to emulate Robertson, Morris, and Park.

ABOVE *Cape Kidnappers, New Zealand—an example of the work of American designer Tom Doak. Doak has an unerring talent for locating stunning green sites and keeping the golfer thinking until the very last putt has dropped.*

FOLLOWING PAGES *The humps and hollows of the Old Course, St. Andrews. The crumpled fairways give all manner of different lies and stances, while bunkers litter the place, very often in the most unexpected of places.*

Courses 1–27

SCOTLAND
1 St. Andrews (Old), Fife
2 Boat of Garten, Inverness-shire
3 Carnoustie, Angus
4 Gleneagles, Perthshire
5 Kingsbarns, Fife
6 Loch Lomond, Dunbartonshire
7 Muirfield, East Lothian
8 Royal Dornoch, Sutherland
9 Royal Troon, Ayrshire
10 Turnberry, Ayrshire

ENGLAND
11 The Belfry, Warwickshire
12 Ganton, Yorkshire
13 Royal Birkdale, Merseyside
14 Royal Liverpool, Cheshire
15 Royal Lytham & St. Annes, Lancashire
16 Royal St. George's, Kent
17 Sunningdale, Surrey
18 Wentworth, Surrey
19 Woodhall Spa, Lincolnshire

WALES
20 Celtic Manor, Gwent
21 Pennard, West Glamorgan

NORTHERN IRELAND
22 Royal County Down, Co. Down
23 Royal Portrush, Co. Antrim

REPUBLIC OF IRELAND
24 Ballybunion, Co. Kerry
25 The K Club, Co. Kildare
26 Lahinch, Co. Clare
27 Old Head, Co. Cork

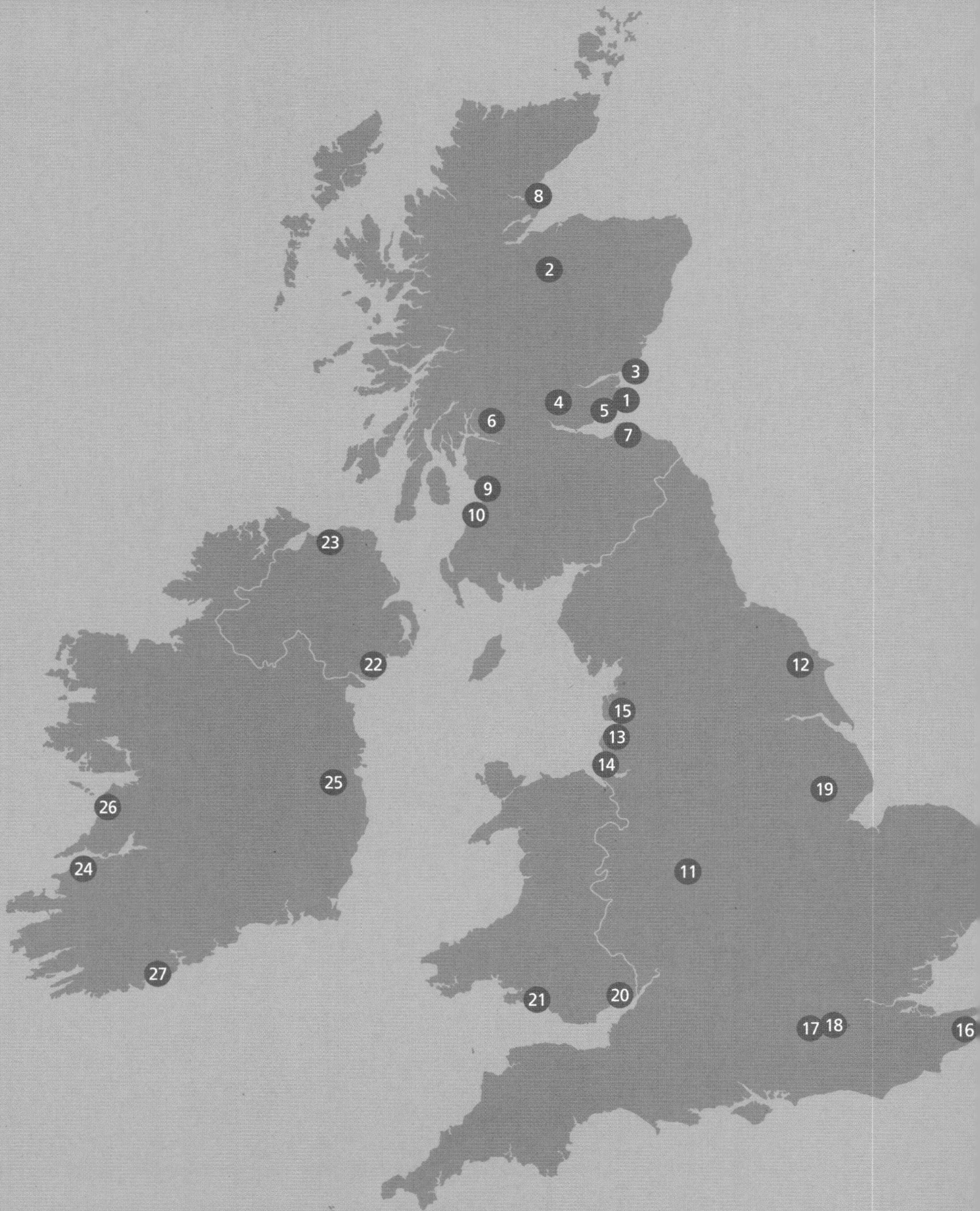

Great Britain & Ireland

Scotland is the cradle of golf. The game was enjoyed there in the Middle Ages, and it is recorded that golf was played in England in 1608 by Scots attached to the court of King James I of England (James VI of Scotland) at Blackheath. However, golf in the British Isles must be judged by the courses of the 21st century, of which there are about 3,000.

Some of these are historic: the Old Course at St. Andrews, Royal Liverpool, Royal County Down. Some are state of the art: Celtic Manor, the Belfry, the K Club. But it is the quality of the courses that do not make the "Top 10 Charts" that illustrates the strength in depth of golf courses in the U.K. and Ireland.

Nowhere in the world can boast finer—or more profuse—links or heathland courses. Yet there are so many other choice terrains—downland, fenland, moorland, and ancestral parkland. For the most part these have been exploited by the great architects of the Golden Age: Harry Colt, Alister MacKenzie, Herbert Fowler, George Abercromby, Tom Simpson. Contemporary giants have not been slow in following suit.

1

St. Andrews

St. Andrews

The Old Course, St. Andrews, Fife, Scotland

There is no more famous golfing town than St. Andrews. It is, after all, the Home of Golf, and the game has been played there since the 15th century. Overlooking the Old Course is the handsome clubhouse of the Royal and Ancient Golf Club (R&A), a comparative newcomer to St. Andrews having been founded in 1754. Nowadays the R&A governs the game throughout the world, with the exception of North America, and every five years it brings its Open Championship (or British Open, as it is widely known through the golfing world) to the Old Course, producing winners of the caliber of Tiger Woods, Jack Nicklaus, Severiano Ballesteros, and Nick Faldo in recent years and James Braid and Bob Jones in the distant past.

Jones was one of many golfers who found that it takes time to appreciate the many subtleties of the Old Course. It has humps and hollows here, there, and everywhere; hundreds of bunkers, many in the unlikeliest of places, some such as Hell, Strath, Hill, or Road terrifying even the world's greats; huge, rolling greens, all but four of them double greens shared by holes playing in opposite directions; and there is a wealth of history in every blade of grass—all the greats of golf have played here, and the locals will recount tales fantastical of derring-do and catastrophe everywhere on the course. The first-time visitor would be well advised to employ the services of a good local caddie, not only to unravel the mysteries of playing the Old Course but also to share in some of those numerous St. Andrews legends.

BOB JONES AND ST. ANDREWS

Strange to relate, Bob Jones hated the Old Course on his first visit, tearing up his card during the 1921 British Open, but he came to love it as he got to know it better, eventually saying, "I could take out of my life everything except my experiences at St. Andrews and I'd still have a rich, full life."

It was on the Old Course in 1930 that Jones won the Amateur Championship, defeating Roger Wethered 7 and 6. In this remarkable year Jones also won the U.S. Amateur at Merion, the U.S. Open at Interlachen and the British Open at Royal Liverpool, a feat unlikely to be repeated, now referred to as the Impregnable Quadrilateral.

At the end of that season Jones, at the age of 28, retired from competitive golf, concentrating on his career as a lawyer.

CARD OF THE COURSE

Hole	Distance (yards)	Par
1	376	4
2	453	4
3	397	4
4	480	4
5	568	5
6	412	4
7	390	4
8	175	3
9	352	4
Out	3,603	36
10	380	4
11	174	3
12	348	4
13	465	4
14	618	5
15	456	4
16	423	4
17	455	4
18	357	4
In	3,676	36
Total	**7,279**	**72**

In the footsteps of the great

There is no simpler drive in golf than that on the 1st hole of the Old Course, or that would be the case if the tee were anywhere else than right in front of the R&A clubhouse. But it is a hugely broad fairway shared with the 18th, and there are no bunkers. However, there is the sinuous Swilcan Burn to be cleared to reach the green. Thereafter the course makes its way out in the shape of a shepherd's crook to the Eden Estuary, turning in a loop before retracing its steps alongside the outward holes on wide shared fairways and greens. The space, which appears to invite uninhibited driving and cavalier approach play, is deceptive. Such are the ingenuities of the course's defenses that how the hole is played from tee to green depends on exactly where the pin is located.

However much you may be enjoying your round you cannot relax until you have passed the 17th, the Road Hole, dominated by the treacherous Road bunker. Get in there and there may be no escape! But all is surely alleviated by the walk up the 18th, the most famous walk in golf.

LEFT *One of the most famous views in golf, looking over the Swilcan Bridge towards the clubhouse of the R&A.*

BELOW RIGHT *The Road bunker is one of the most feared on the Old Course. Many great players settle for a bogey five rather than risk failing to escape its clutches.*

"Without a doubt, I like it best of all the Open venues. It is my favorite course in the world."

TIGER WOODS, BRITISH OPEN CHAMPION AT ST. ANDREWS IN 2000 AND 2005

1

BUNKERS—THE STORIES BEHIND THE NAMES

It is said that there are 112 bunkers on the Old Course, which seems a conservative estimate to anyone who has played there. Some of them are in such obscure places that you could never imagine golfers getting into them—but they have! Most also have names. These are some of the more colorful:

CHEAPE'S (2ND HOLE) Named after the Cheape family that owns the nearby Strathtyrum estate. Sir James Cheape bought the Old Course in 1821 to save it from rabbit farmers. His son later sold it to the R&A, which, in turn, sold it to the town. Golfers owe Sir James an enormous debt of gratitude.

CARTGATE (3RD HOLE) Shares its name with the hole itself, so called because of the former cart track that crossed the hole toward the beach.

GINGER BEER (4TH HOLE) Again, a name shared with the hole, referring back to the mid-19th century when "Old Daw" Anderson set up a ginger beer stall there.

SUTHERLAND (4TH/15TH HOLE) Sutherland should not be a factor on the 4th were it not for the difficulties of the right-hand side of the fairway often forcing golfers too far to the left. It was named after one A. G. Sutherland, who is reputed to have had the bunker re-excavated when it was filled in in the 1860s.

COTTAGE (4TH/15TH HOLE) For the same reasons as Sutherland, Cottage should not be a factor on the 4th, but it is. It refers to Pilmour Cottage, which once stood nearby and is now the clubhouse of the Eden Course.

STUDENTS (4TH HOLE) There are two theories behind the naming of these bunkers. It has been said that they refer to the practice of busy students, not having the time for a full round, playing out this far and then turning for home. An alternative suggestion is that these were cosy (and out-of-sight) places for male students to take their lady friends.

SPECTACLES (4TH HOLE) This is exactly what they look like, set at the foot of the ridge crossing this fairway.

COFFINS (6TH/13TH HOLES) You are playing a little extravagantly if you get in these on the 6th hole. They are a threat to all, however, on the 13th. They are so coffin-like that you feel you may be in them forever.

SHELL (7TH HOLE) Apart from the fact that it looks rather like a mussel shell from above, the name refers back to the days when the base of the bunker used to be cockle shells. (If you are wildly off course on the 7th, you might find yourself in Hill or Strath bunkers—leave these for the 11th!)

SHORT HOLE BUNKER (8TH HOLE) Some of the bunker names are rather more prosaic!

KRUGER (9TH HOLE) This is actually two bunkers, built during the Boer War and named after the former president of the Transvaal. A third bunker, further on, is named Mrs. Kruger. Rumor has it that there is also one named Kruger's Mistress!

STRATH (11TH HOLE) This commemorates the Strath brothers. Andrew won the 1865 British Open. His brother David tied for first place in 1876 but he refused to take part in the play-off, leaving Bob Martin as the champion.

HILL (11TH HOLE) Hill is not far behind Strath in venom. It is cut into the face of the hill on which the 11th green sits.

ADMIRAL'S (12TH HOLE) Sited close to the tee, the bunker is said to have been named after an admiral who, in his 80s, failed to see the sizable bunker as he walked forward from the tee, distracted as he was by a beautiful young lady walking past, wearing, it is said, pillar-box red.

BELOW *Hell Bunker dominates strategy on the 14th hole for handicap golfers. Will the second shot clear it or do you go round the side of it?*

STROKE (12TH HOLE) Get in here and you almost certainly will drop a stroke.

NICK'S (13TH HOLE) The first of several bunkers threatening a pulled drive, presumably named after the devil who put it there.

CAT'S TRAP (13TH HOLE) Invisible from the fairway, the bunker catches your ball as a cat traps a mouse.

WALKINSHAW (13TH HOLE) Named after a local golfer who made a habit of visiting this pot bunker.

LION'S MOUTH (13TH HOLE) Lion's Mouth is another vicious bunker lying in wait beyond Cat's Trap. Perversely, Lion's Mouth is smaller than Cat's Trap.

THE BEARDIES (14TH HOLE) A quartet of bunkers with whiskery grass adorning their lips.

BENTY (14TH HOLE) Benty refers to one of the traditional seaside grasses: Bent.

KITCHEN (14TH HOLE) Kitchen was once known as the Devil's Kitchen because it was a small but deep pot bunker. It has since been enlarged.

HELL (14TH HOLE) One of the best-known bunkers in golf with a vast acreage and a seriously steep face from which escape forward is by no means guaranteed.

GRAVE (14TH HOLE) A small bunker in front of the green, which was formerly coffin-shaped.

PRINCIPAL'S NOSE (16TH HOLE) A set of three bunkers said to represent the prominent nose of the principal of St. Mary's College in the mid-19th century. It is also said to be named after the ugly protuberance from the porch above the doorway of a principal's lodgings in the town.

DEACON SIME (16TH HOLE) Deacon Sime refers to a St. Andrews clergyman who asked for his ashes to be scattered in the bunker, on the premise that he had spent so much of his earthly life in that particular bunker that he might as well spend eternity there as well.

GRANT'S (16TH HOLE) Commemorates a 19th-century captain of the R&A who made a habit of getting into this bunker.

WIG (16TH HOLE) Formerly called Jackson's Wig, recalling the formal dress of golfers in days past. Jackson was a captain of the R&A.

SCHOLAR'S (17TH HOLE) Scholar's is a reminder that the course used to be played in the opposite direction. You were a promising young scholar if you could clear this bunker with your drive.

PROGRESSING (17TH HOLE) You were doing well, but had not yet attained the proficiency of a scholar, if you could clear this bunker.

ROAD (17TH HOLE) The fearsome bunker that eats into the green of the Road Hole, both named after the tarmac road running tight along the right side of the green.

Boat of Garten

Boat of Garten Golf and Tennis Club, Inverness-shire, Scotland

Rarely is golf played in a more beautiful setting than at Boat of Garten. The Cairngorm Mountains provide a breathtaking backdrop before which ribbons of crumpled fairways are threaded through avenues of silver birches, with abundant heather and broom adding swathes of purple and brilliant gold to the more restrained greens and blues of the mountains and Abernethy Forest. Deer and the occasional osprey remind us that this part of Scotland is particularly rich in wildlife, while the puffing of a steam engine on the preserved Strathspey Railway brings a period touch to this very unspoiled corner of the Highlands.

ABOVE *With the backdrop of the Cairngorm Mountains, Boat of Garten is undeniably pretty. It is also immense fun at whatever level you play. This is the 2nd hole.*

In fact it was the coming of the railway in 1863 that put Boat of Garten on the map. The hamlet of Gart, with its ferry across the River Spey, already existed there. The station built to serve the village and ferry took its name, Boat of Garten, from that ferry. With easier access the village grew into a popular retreat for walkers, anglers, and those who valued the crystal-clear mountain air (and, more recently, skiers). It was only a matter of time before there was a golf course.

Modest beginnings

At first, in 1898, the golf course was a simple layout of six holes. A couple of extra holes and tennis courts were constructed later. In due course further land became available, and James Braid was called in to advise on a full 18-hole course. It opened in 1932 and remains almost the same today apart from the recent conversion of two former par 4s into par 5s. Braid was then one of the most sought-after

architects in golf course design and had demonstrated with his alterations to Carnoustie in 1926 that he could produce a course to examine even the world's best players. At 5,876 yards/5,373 m from the very tips, "Boat" is hardly a championship test, yet it is not a pushover for accomplished golfers. The charm of Braid's course is its subtlety, but sloppy golf is rigorously punished, with heather waiting to swallow careless tee shots, well-placed bunkers and many a drop-off to the sides or behind the greens.

Unusually, Boat opens with a short hole. It would normally present no difficulty, but a touch of uncertainty is understandable on the first shot of the day. A straightforward par 4 and another short hole take play to the course boundary, on the other side of which runs the Strathspey Railway. From here on the fairways take on a mischievous, rolling character, often demanding of the golfer the ability to play with the ball above or below the feet from a rising or a hanging lie. The 6th is a particularly fine hole, with a long, slow curving fairway calling for excellent judgment of length and direction from the tee and a green raised above bunkers demanding a perfect second shot. Braid himself championed the 12th hole, perhaps the most handsome of all the holes. Boat keeps one of its toughest holes for the last, with a very testing approach shot to a raised green. After the round, there are few better views to be enjoyed from a clubhouse than those at Boat.

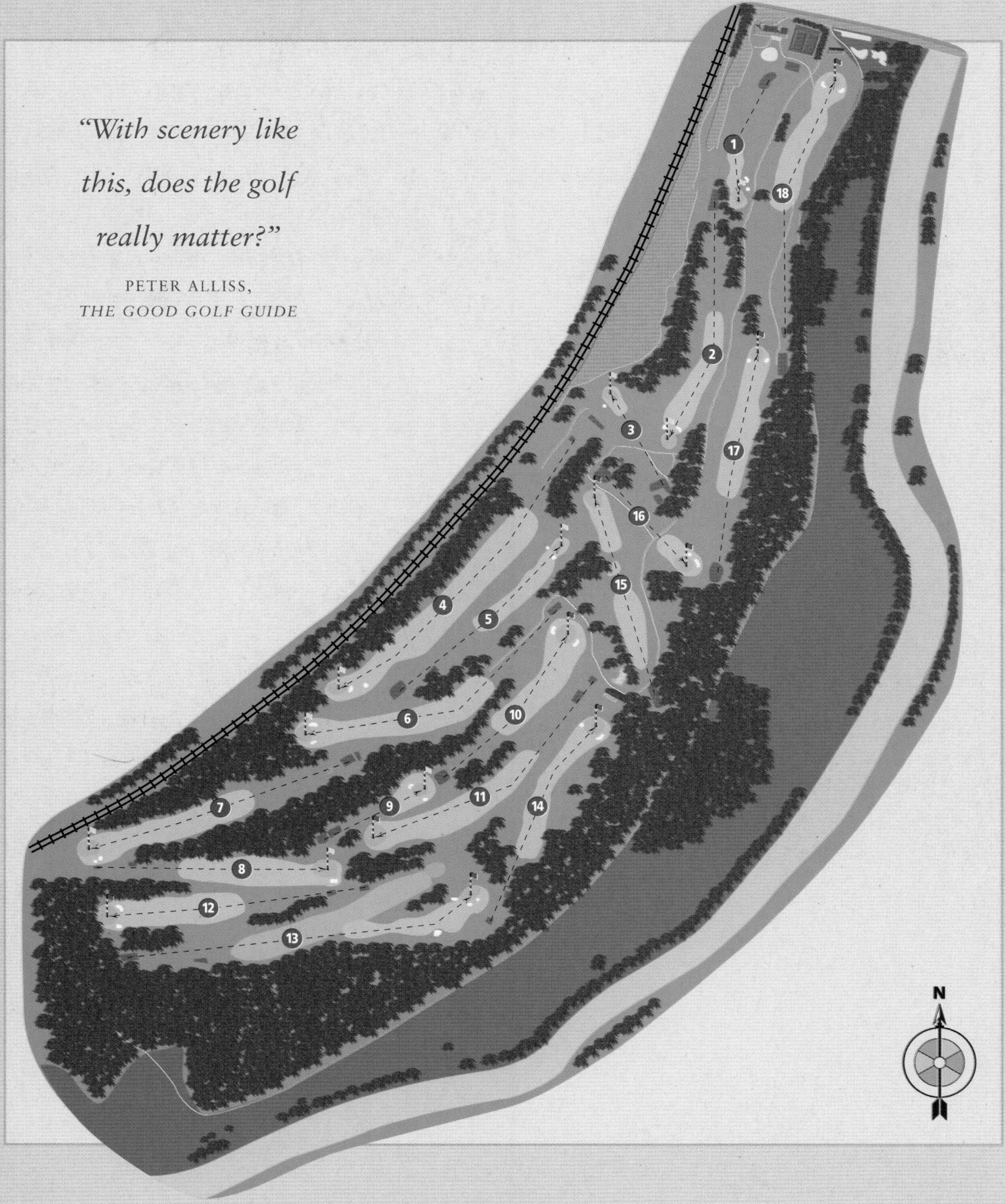

"With scenery like this, does the golf really matter?"

PETER ALLISS,
THE GOOD GOLF GUIDE

CARD OF THE COURSE

Hole	*Distance (yards)*	*Par*
1	189	3
2	360	4
3	163	3
4	514	5
5	301	4
6	403	4
7	386	4
8	355	4
9	154	3
Out	2,825	34
10	271	4
11	379	4
12	349	4
13	473	5
14	323	4
15	307	4
16	168	3
17	344	4
18	437	4
In	3,051	36
Total	**5,876**	**70**

3

Carnoustie

Carnoustie

Championship Course, Carnoustie Golf Links, Angus, Scotland

Is Carnoustie the toughest course on the British Open roster? How it was prepared for the 1999 Open in the wind and rain it certainly was, Paul Lawrie's winning score being six over par. It was more sympathetically prepared for the 2007 Open, when Padraig Harrington and Sergio Garcia tied on 277, seven under par, Harrington winning in a four-hole play-off. What most observers were agreed on was that this set-up displayed all the greatness of this historic links, and in particular that there were often two or three different strategies for playing a particular hole, depending on a golfer's strengths and weaknesses, the wind and the weather.

It is not certain when golf began in Carnoustie (probably over 500 years ago) but it was some time around 1842 that Allan Robertson—the pre-eminent golfer at that time—was brought from St. Andrews to lay out a ten-hole course on the Barry Links. Another St. Andrews stalwart, Old Tom Morris, made considerable alterations in 1867, expanding the course to 18 holes, and James Braid made the final significant changes in 1926.

The longest British Open course

Carnoustie hosted its first British Open in 1931, with Scottish-born American Tommy Armour coming from five behind to win—subsequent champions have included Henry Cotton (1937), Ben Hogan (1953), Gary Player (1963), and Tom Watson (1975). As a championship course Carnoustie has always been among the longest. For the 2007 Open it measured a daunting 7,412 yards/6,778 m, the longest ever, with two par 4s reaching almost 500 yards/457 m in length, yet such is the prowess of contemporary professionals with modern equipment that many forsook their drivers, taking long irons from the tee. They did it for the simple reason that you cannot blast your way round this course. You have to plot your way around it. The bunkers are deep, gathering and perfectly positioned; the rough can be savage; out-of-bounds threatens on several holes; and the Jockie's and Barry burns were brilliantly incorporated into the design, especially on the last two holes.

Jockie's Burn, for instance, limits the length of the tee shot on the challenging 5th, putting pressure on the approach to a multi-level, snaking green, cunningly

LEFT *Barry Burn, snaking across the 17th and 18th. Jean van de Velde's skirmishes with it cost him a seven in the 1999 British Open, when a six would have won it.*

bunkered and over 50 yards/46 m deep. Out-of-bounds waits to wreck scores on the long 6th, causing many an errant tee shot to be pushed into the deep rough on the other side.

Of all the hazards it is the Barry Burn that is most feared, very largely because it comes into play viciously on the last two holes, hard on the heels of the 16th, a seriously long par 3 on which only the straightest of tee shots can pierce the bunkered mounds guarding the front of the green. Birdies here are rare, dropped shots frequent. The 17th then strikes out over the burn, which meanders hugely, creating almost an island fairway, with length restricted where the burn crosses the fairway.

Still to come is the scariest drive of them all, back over the Barry Burn to another narrow fairway, once again bounded by the burn. Even after a successful drive, there remains the long second to the green, which lies perilously close to the out-of-bounds fence and is, naturally, only just beyond yet another meander of the dreaded burn. What a tough hole!

CARD OF THE COURSE

Hole	*Distance (yards)*	*Par*
1	406	4
2	463	4
3	358	4
4	412	4
5	415	4
6	578	5
7	410	4
8	183	3
9	478	4
Out	3,703	36
10	466	4
11	383	4
12	499	4
13	176	3
14	514	5
15	472	4
16	248	3
17	461	4
18	499	4
In	3,718	35
Total	**7,421**	**71**

▸ Almost 300 young men from Carnoustie and the surrounding area have emigrated to the United States to work as golf professionals. One of the best known was Stewart Maiden, Bob Jones's teacher at the East Lake Club, Atlanta.

▸ The Smith brothers from Carnoustie had an enviable professional record. Alex was twice U.S. Open champion, Willie once, and Macdonald came second to Bob Jones in both the British Open and the U.S. Open in 1930.

▸ Ben Hogan, one of golf's all-time greats, entered only one British Open, in 1953 at Carnoustie. He won the championship by four strokes. It was part of a remarkable run of victories that included the U.S. Masters and the U.S. Open.

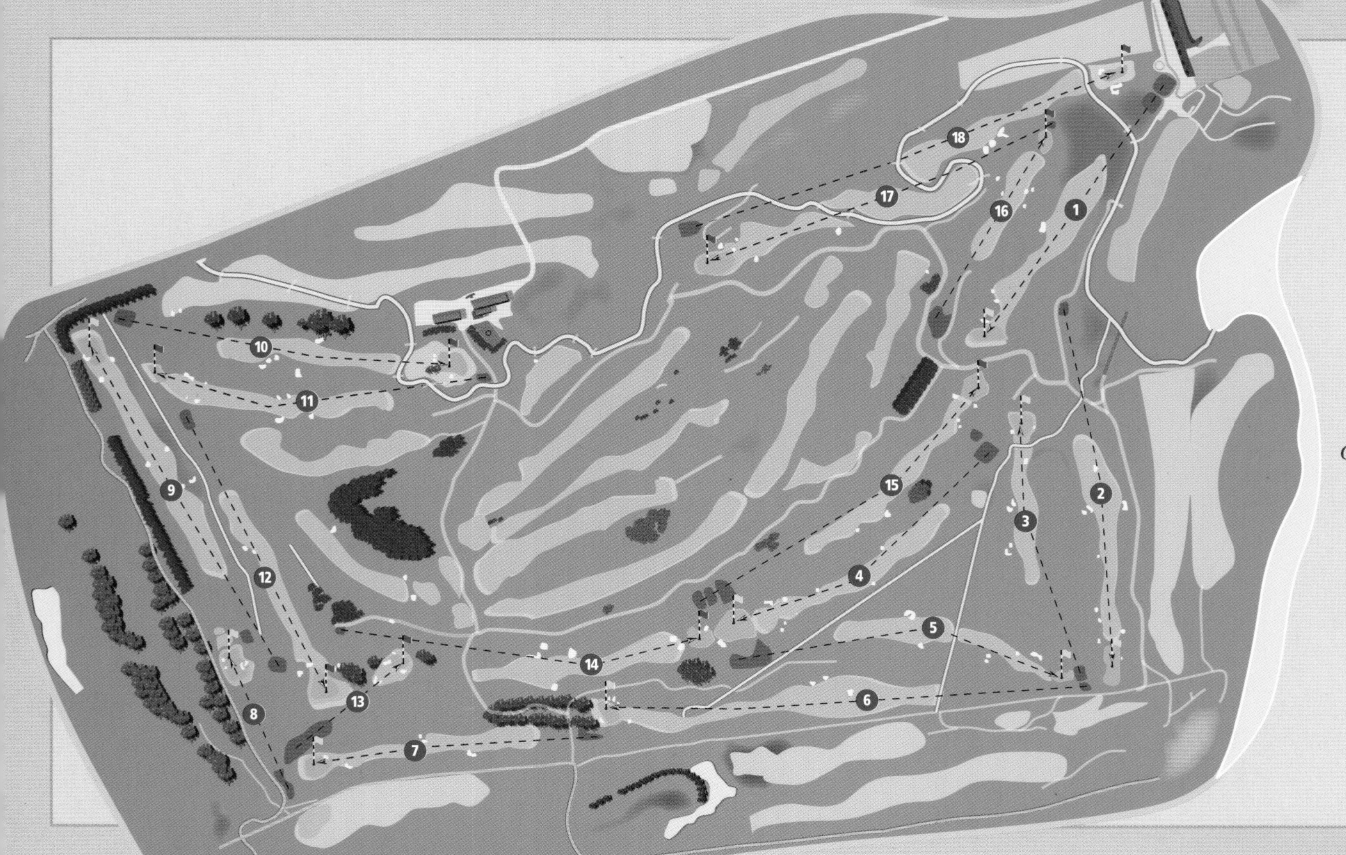

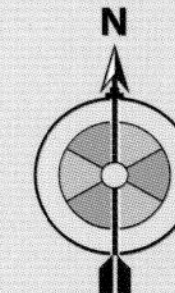

"I love playing over here because it allows you to be creative."

TIGER WOODS

Gleneagles

King's Course, Gleneagles Hotel, Auchterarder, Perthshire, Scotland

When the 2014 Ryder Cup is played in Scotland it will be at Gleneagles. Jack Nicklaus's PGA Centenary Course has the honor of hosting it, having proved its fitness by hosting the annual Johnnie Walker Championship on the European Tour. The enormous hotel, built in the style of a French château and the venue for the 2005 G8 Summit, will then be exactly 90 years old.

ABOVE *The 7th on the King's Course is a tough dogleg, on which the further you aim left to shorten the dogleg the longer you have to drive to clear a ridge.*

Older still are James Braid's two wonderful courses, opened before the hotel, in 1919. The King's and Queen's courses were a vital part of the strategy to attract royalty, nobility, and the merely wealthy to the hotel, the pride and joy of the Caledonian Railway, which was described both as a "Palace in the Glens" and as the "Riviera in the Highlands." Clearly the company's ambitions were well founded, for the hotel remains one of the world's great hotels to this day, and Braid's golf courses are as revered as ever.

Both the King's and the Queen's are serious contenders for the coveted title of the finest inland course in Scotland. Neither course is long enough seriously to challenge today's top players—hence the need for the construction of the PGA Centenary Course—but those who value charm, variety, subtlety, and ingenuity in a golf course in ravishing surroundings can still derive great satisfaction from a round on either, preferably both. And, of course, they are maintained in impeccable condition.

▶ The principal reason for the wonderful condition of the courses at Gleneagles is that they were built on the sand and gravel left behind when the ice from the Ice Age melted.

▶ "The finest parcel of land in the world I have ever been given to work with," is how Jack Nicklaus described the building of the PGA Centenary Course, venue for the 2014 Ryder Cup.

CARD OF THE COURSE

Hole	Distance (yards)	Par
1	362	4
2	436	4
3	374	4
4	466	4
5	178	3
6	480	5
7	444	4
8	178	3
9	409	4
Out	3,327	35
10	499	5
11	230	3
12	442	4
13	464	4
14	309	4
15	459	4
16	158	3
17	377	4
18	525	5
In	3,463	36
Total	6,790	71

Drum Sichty and Kittle Kink

On both courses each hole is named, an old Scottish tradition, and at Gleneagles the holes were named from the outset, not carrying forward some ancient traditional name (for the holes were new) but quite simply to amuse visitors. For the record, "Drum Sichty" is no more than a view of the hills while "Kittle Kink" is a tricky bend. But the names are good ice-breakers between player and caddie, and a good caddie is useful not only in guiding the player through the many problems posed by hilly courses, but also in sharing the finer points of Braid's clever designs with the appreciative golfer.

One of the great delights of the courses is the way the holes follow each other to create an integrated whole, with refreshing change of pace, a good balance of challenges, and a constant sense of development. At a little under 6,000 yards/5,486 m the Queen's Course may seem too short for the accomplished player, but do not be fooled! Seven of the par 4s exceed 400 yards/366 m in length and there are two substantial par 3s, the 14th and 17th. It was a favorite course of Lee Trevino.

In comparison with the Queen's, the King's is said to be more masculine. Sandy Lyle has particular respect for the tough, uphill 4th: in Lyle's opinion, "a first-class hole by any standard." Braid himself considered his favorite hole on the course to be the 13th, another long two-shot hole, appropriately named Braid's Brawest ("Braid's Best"). Everywhere there is a sense of space, the twists and turns of each course giving ever-changing views of the uplifting mountain scenery. These are not so much golf courses as experiences!

"If heaven is as good as this, I sure hope they have some tee times left."

LEE TREVINO, REMARKING ON THE QUEEN'S COURSE

Kingsbarns

Kingsbarns

Kingsbarns Golf Links, St. Andrews, Fife, Scotland

"Let it not be difficult for the sake of being difficult; rather, let it be interesting and engaging." These are the thoughts of Mark Parsinen, one of the developers of the new course at Kingsbarns, 6 miles/10 km south of St. Andrews on the Fife coast. It has already made a big impression on players and spectators during the annual Dunhill Links Championship, which is played over the three venues of Carnoustie, Kingsbarns, and St. Andrews. There are even calls for it to be added to the British Open roster, which is unlikely given its proximity to St. Andrews.

Although the modern Kingsbarns course was opened as recently as 2000, golf has been played here since 1793. That original course was abandoned in the mid-19th century and turned into farmland. Another course was laid out in 1922, but it, too, foundered when the site was mined to deter invasion at the outbreak of World War II. After the war the land reverted to farming use. Those earlier courses were humble affairs, none being on the scale of today's state-of-the-art Kingsbarns, which is undeniably impressive.

Recreating a links

The architect charged with laying out the new course was an American, Kyle Phillips, working in partnership with Parsinen. He was faced with a mammoth task, for part of the site available was silt and clay, and a great deal of earthmoving was required to redistribute the deep sands from the eastern side of the land equally throughout the course, to build sand dunes from scratch, and to provide rapid-draining soil for the fairways. The views inland from

LEFT *The 12th curves in a long arc beside the beach, which forms part of the Fife Coastal Path.*

BELOW *Golfers on the 15th green, a fine par 3 running hard against the shore.*

the course are nothing special over flattish farmland, so Phillips decided to orientate the course in such a way that the majority of holes would enjoy seascapes, and that those holes that play away from the sea would have dunes or trees as a backdrop. At Kingsbarns the visual aspect of the course is as impressive as the golfing challenge it presents.

On an exposed site such as this the wind is rarely absent, and Phillips allowed for this by providing wide fairways that are themselves a clever part in the design as they offer multiple choices—there are many different ways of playing most holes, depending on the skill of the player and his or her intelligence. Kingsbarns is, then, a welcome change from so many one-dimensional, penal, contemporary designs that call for a specific, perfectly executed stroke on every shot and, thus, leave no opportunities for invention and individuality.

As early as the first drive of the round a choice can be made, the harder drive to the left leaving an easier approach to the green and vice versa. And what a green it is, seemingly perched on a cliff hanging over the sea! In fact it is one of Phillips's many optical illusions. There is room for several further holes below the green. Nor did Phillips miss any opportunity to route the course along the sea shore, with no fewer than six holes enjoying close proximity to breaking waves. One of those is the majestic 12th, one of the most photographed holes on the links, its curving fairway hugging the rocks and strands for some 600 yards/549 m—a fine golf hole in a magical setting.

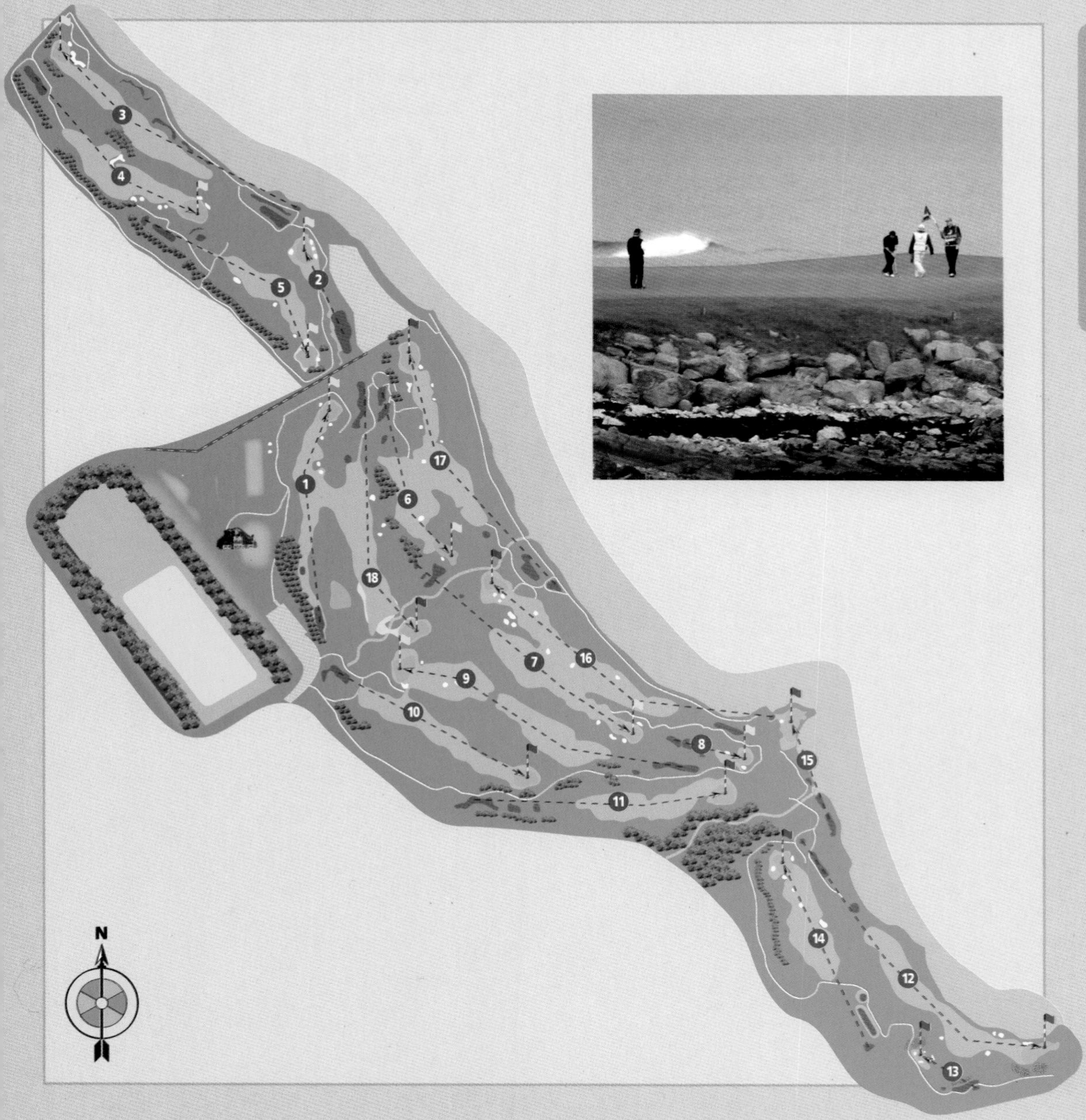

CARD OF THE COURSE

Hole	Distance (yards)	Par
1	414	4
2	200	3
3	516	5
4	408	4
5	398	4
6	337	4
7	470	4
8	168	3
9	558	5
Out	3,469	36
10	387	4
11	455	4
12	606	5
13	148	3
14	366	4
15	212	3
16	565	5
17	474	4
18	444	4
In	3,657	36
Total	**7,126**	**72**

Loch Lomond

Loch Lomond

Loch Lomond Golf Club, Luss by Alexandria, Dunbartonshire, Scotland

Every year, in the week before the British Open, eyes turn to Loch Lomond, home of the Scottish Open since 1996. Many of the great names of golf take part in this championship to hone their games for the British Open. To others it represents their last chance to qualify for the big one. For the spectators—and millions who watch on television—it is a rare opportunity to revel in the romantic setting of this very private golf course, set in the historic parkland on the banks of Loch Lomond.

A troubled birth

Loch Lomond was not an instant success. It took years before planning permission was granted and construction could begin. No sooner had ex-Open champion Tom Weiskopf and his design partner, Jay Morrish, completed the course than a recession hit and the receivers were called in. The grass lay fallow. Enter Arizona businessman Lyle Anderson. Weiskopf persuaded him to visit the dormant course. Anderson liked what he saw and agreed to back the venture with cash—lots of it! He now presides over an international club with lavishly appointed facilities, boasting a range of country pursuits, and with two top-class golf courses (the other being Dundonald on the Ayrshire coast).

Eye candy is the bane of much contemporary golf architecture, but at Loch Lomond Weiskopf and Morrish had no need to resort to it. The place is ravishing in its own right and the architects used the mountain and loch vistas superbly, also utilizing the streams and ponds, marshes, and woodlands as principal elements in the strategy of design. On the 13th, for instance, there is no sight of the Loch, so a funnel of trees is used to lead the eye from the elevated tee along the well-bunkered fairway of this fine par 5, then beyond up into the heather-clad hills.

This is followed by a great spectator hole, the drivable par-4 14th. The safe play is out to the left, on to a fairway with an iron for position, then a simple pitch over a stream and bunker to the green. The daring play is an all-or-nothing shot over a treacherous bog, either on to the green for an eagle putt, or into the bog with a bogey looming.

These are part of a glorious finish, the 17th being a well-defended short hole, and the last hole a strong dogleg where risk-taking is well rewarded, but failure is wretched.

RIGHT *There have been three holes-in-one on Loch Lomond's 17th during the Bell's Scottish Open: Jarmo Sandelin and Mathias Grönberg in 2000 and Peter Lonard in 2003.*

The fairest of tests

The course is well respected by top players, particularly for its fairness—there is very little blindness and there are few capricious bounces. It is a notably good test of driving, the rough being particularly grasping, and some of its bunkering can only be described as ferocious! Perhaps of all the Open courses Muirfield has no "stand-out" hole, for it is a very evenly distributed examination of the game, but most players would agree that the 6th, 8th, and 18th are among the best long, two-shot holes in links golf. The 13th, too, is a white-knuckle short hole with a long, narrow green perched above five terrifying bunkers. A brilliant escape from one of these set up Ernie Els's British Open win in 2002.

From the visitor's point of view, it is worth noting that the club does not introduce temporary tees or winter greens in the off season. You get to play the real course, and for a reduced green fee, to boot.

CARD OF THE COURSE

Hole	Distance (yards)	Par
1	448	4
2	351	4
3	378	4
4	213	3
5	560	5
6	468	4
7	185	3
8	443	4
9	508	5
Out	3,554	36
10	475	4
11	389	4
12	381	4
13	191	3
14	448	4
15	415	4
16	186	3
17	546	5
18	449	4
In	3,480	35
Total	**7,034**	**71**

Jack Nicklaus, after winning the 1966 British Open, said, "It is essentially a fair course. It has more definition than any links that the Open is played on." He went on to name the first course he created—in Dublin, Ohio, USA—Muirfield Village.

It was at Muirfield, in 1892, that the British Open was first played over 72 holes. Previously it had been over 36 holes. It was also at Muirfield in 1892 that an entrance fee to play in the British Open was first imposed.

Ben Crenshaw (former U.S. Masters champion and a distinguished golf course architect) praised Muirfield for "its beautiful honesty as a test of golf."

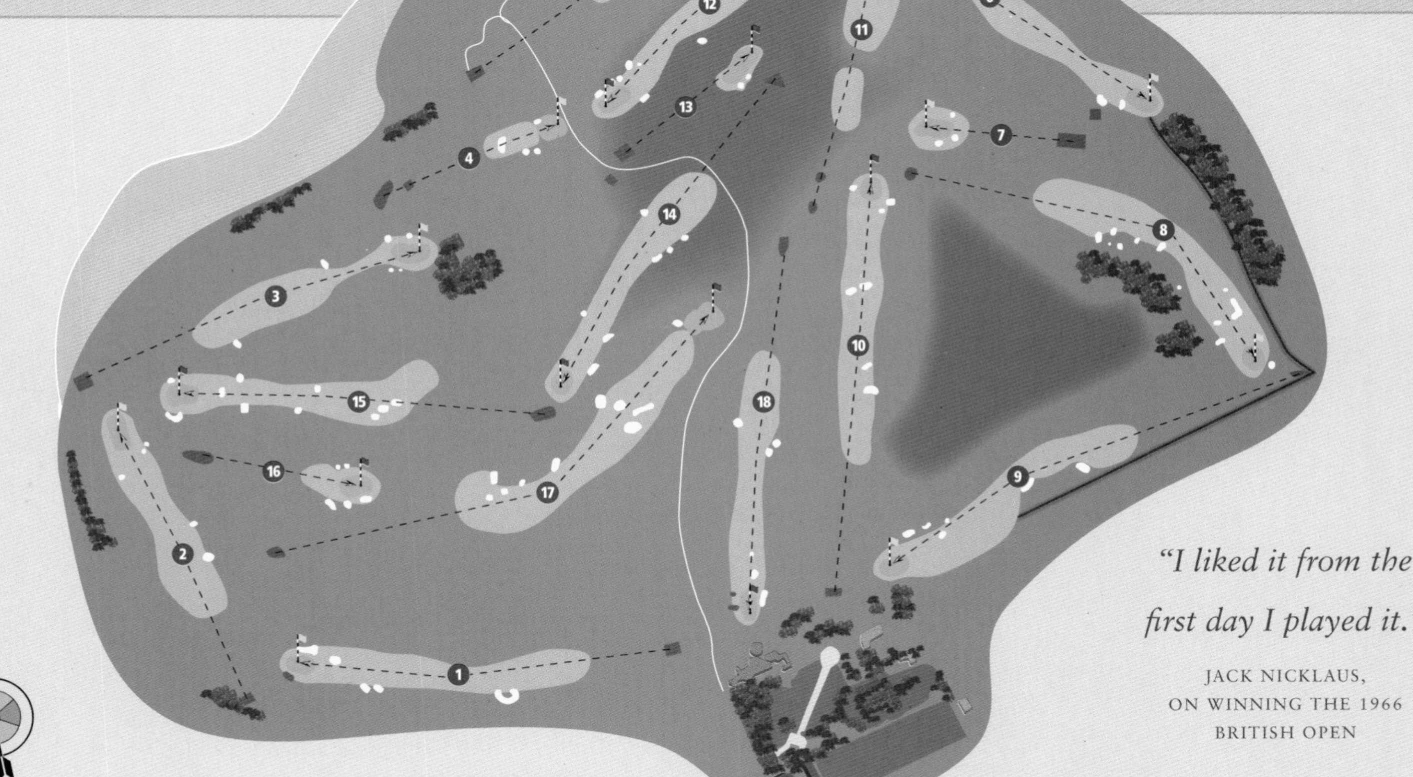

"I liked it from the first day I played it."

JACK NICKLAUS, ON WINNING THE 1966 BRITISH OPEN

Royal Dornoch

Royal Dornoch Golf Club, Dornoch, Sutherland, Scotland

"The most fun I ever had playing golf," was Tom Watson's opinion of Royal Dornoch, an opinion shared by many of the famous golfers who have made the pilgrimage north to Dornoch. They have visited in large numbers because Dornoch is high on the must-play list of all who have an interest in golf course design.

Golf has been played at Dornoch for some 500 years. The present club, with a modest nine-hole course, was founded in 1877, but a more significant date in Dornoch's development was 1883, when John Sutherland was appointed secretary. He it was who brought in Old Tom Morris to extend the course to 18 holes in 1886; who subsequently refined and improved the design; who had the course brought into exemplary condition; who worked to have Dornoch created a Royal club; and who promoted Dornoch in his writings for London periodicals. Sutherland involved his professionals and greenkeepers in the development of the course and one of those was Donald Ross, who subsequently emigrated to the United States where he introduced the concept of Dornoch-style raised greens to American golf design.

Remoteness is a blessing for Dornoch

Because Dornoch is so far from large centers of population it has never hosted important professional tournaments or the British Open. For that reason the course has been spared the incessant lengthening and alterations that are deemed necessary to keep modern professionals in check. Its holes remain as they were intended to be played twenty, thirty, or even fifty years ago, and the visitor today is still required to utilize a whole variety of types of pitch shot to gain access to these brilliantly sited greens. But it is not only on the approach shot that intelligent play is demanded, for the fairways use the natural slopes, humps, and hollows cleverly, calling for precise and thoughtful driving. The wind, too, must be taken into account.

RIGHT *The delightful 10th hole at Dornoch, a gentle enough par 3 if you find the green from the tee, but the very devil if you miss.*

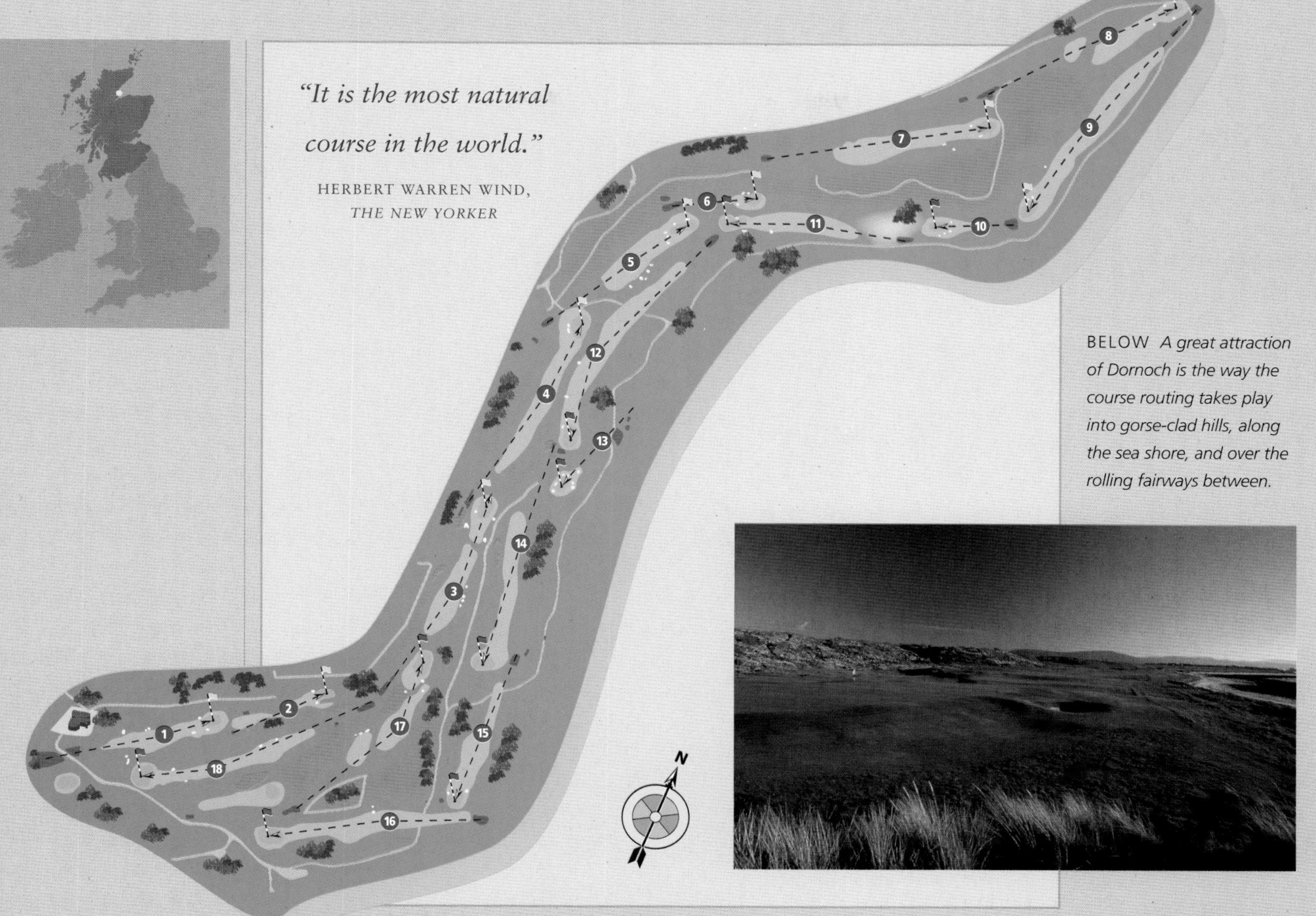

"It is the most natural course in the world."

HERBERT WARREN WIND, *THE NEW YORKER*

BELOW *A great attraction of Dornoch is the way the course routing takes play into gorse-clad hills, along the sea shore, and over the rolling fairways between.*

CARD OF THE COURSE

Hole	*Distance (yards)*	*Par*	*Hole*	*Distance (yards)*	*Par*
1	331	4	10	177	3
2	184	3	11	450	4
3	414	4	12	507	5
4	427	4	13	180	3
5	354	4	14	445	4
6	163	3	15	358	4
7	463	4	16	402	4
8	437	4	17	405	4
9	529	5	18	456	4
Out	3,302	35	In	3,380	35
			Total	**6,682**	**70**

Tom Watson's favorite hole is the 5th, a hole that certainly proves that excessive length is not essential for greatness. The view from the elevated tee is encouraging, the wide fairway some way below awaiting the drive. Yet the green is very long and angled significantly from left to right. The ideal drive, then, is down the left, but this is the side where trouble lurks in the form of a hill covered in gorse, threatening a lost ball. On the right the fairway slopes, guiding the ball inexorably toward a run of bunkers. Even if these are avoided the approach shot must be played across the axis of the narrow, kidney-shaped, putting surface, and there are further bunkers awaiting if that shot is overcooked.

Another of Dornoch's great holes is the bunkerless 14th—Foxy. Everything is governed by a series of dunes, which eat into the fairway from the right, obscuring the green from anywhere other than the extreme left of the fairway. The green is tucked round to the right behind the last of the dunes, broad but shallow, and raised sufficiently to make an approach shot from any length difficult to execute. The 17th, too, is a fine hole, sweeping downhill from the tee, then sharply up to a marvellously located green.

THE LURE OF DORNOCH

John Sutherland, the club's first secretary, was a considerable publicist for Dornoch, writing about it in the *London Daily News* and *Golf Illustrated*. But, unlike many of the great Scottish links that were located near railroads, Dornoch had no railroad until 1902. When the line opened, Sutherland lost no time in alerting golfers all over the country to take the overnight sleeper from London, to play the course the following morning. Among those who visited during these years were the Great Triumvirate: James Braid, Harry Vardon, and J. H. Taylor. Taylor was so thrilled by the course that he arranged to take a fortnight's holiday in Dornoch every year while he was at the peak of his career, so perfect was the course for honing his game. Another who visited, much later, was Ben Crenshaw, who came to Dornoch as part of his preparations for the 1980 British Open, held that year at Muirfield. Asked, when he returned to Muirfield, what he thought of Dornoch, he replied, "Let me put it this way, I nearly did not come back."

RIGHT *The 2nd at Dornoch looks benign enough from here, but get in the front right bunker and you may well have to escape sideways or backward.*

Iain Lowe Photography

Royal Troon

Royal Troon Golf Club, Troon, Ayrshire, Scotland

Troon was already an important sea port on the Firth of Clyde when a railroad was opened from Glasgow in 1840. Soon its beaches and clean air attracted Glaswegians to take vacations there and the wealthy to build big houses. The next railroad station south of Troon was Prestwick, the birthplace of championship golf, and in 1878 it was decided that Troon should have its own golf course.

Land was leased from the Duke of Portland and a five-hole course was created in the area of the present 1st, 2nd, 17th, and 18th holes. That course was extended piecemeal and by 1888 there were 18 holes, stretching to 5,600 yards/ 5,121 m, following much the same route as today's course. Further amendments took place over the years and by 1923 Troon was ready to host its first British Open.

Arnold Palmer was at the peak of his career when he won the British Open at Troon in 1962, yet even with his extraordinary powers of recovery he realized that he should "not get locked into a life and death struggle with the course." The first-time visitor, looking down the opening fairway from the tee, could be forgiven for querying that comment, for everything looks so straightforward and benign. And so it is, for a while.

Increasingly menacing

"As much by skill as by strength" is the club's motto, and the first three holes amble gently alongside the beach, each under 400 yards/366 m in length. Two birdieable par 5s are separated by a charming par 3 on top of the dunes, and everything seems pretty simple so far. The most inviting drive of the round follows at the 7th, but already the mind is sharpening for the mischief of the 8th, the notorious Postage

SOCIAL STATUS

At the end of the 1923 British Open the champion, Arthur Havers, and the runner-up, Walter Hagen, were invited into the clubhouse for the presentation ceremony. Hagen refused to go as none of the other professional golfers had been admitted to the clubhouse during the tournament. He went instead to the pub, where a large number of the spectators joined him.

▶ At the age of 71 Gene Sarazen played in the 1973 British Open at Troon and holed his tee shot on the infamous Postage Stamp for an ace in the first round. In the second round he found a bunker off the tee, but then holed his recovery shot.

LEFT *The Postage Stamp was originally played blind to a green on the far side of the dune. The new hole, built in 1909–10, was opened by Harry Vardon, James Braid, J. H. Taylor, and Alex Herd.*

CARD OF THE COURSE

Hole	Distance (yards)	Par
1	361	4
2	391	4
3	379	4
4	558	5
5	210	3
6	599	5
7	403	4
8	123	3
9	423	4
Out	3,447	36
10	438	4
11	488	4
12	431	4
13	470	4
14	178	3
15	481	4
16	542	5
17	222	3
18	453	4
In	3,703	35
Total	**7,150**	**71**

Stamp. It is the shortest hole in British Open golf, but you are either on the minuscule putting surface in one stroke, expecting a birdie, or else, if you missed the green, on a rough-clad hillock, in one of five deep greenside bunkers, or far below the green in a grassy hollow. Escape from any of these is no certainty, as the German player, Hermann Tissies, found to his cost in the 1950 British Open. He finished up with a 15!

It is on the back nine, almost invariably played into the wind, that Troon bares its teeth, starting with an intimidating blind and angled drive to the elusive 10th fairway. The subsequent approach to a pinnacle green is difficult to judge. As for the 11th, it was described by Arnold Palmer as, "The most dangerous hole I have ever seen." The young Jack Nicklaus ran up a 10 on this hole in his first Troon Open, and during the 1997 British Open the hole played to an average of 4.65 shots, easily the hardest on the course. Gorse and the hole's proximity to the railroad track are the principal card wreckers.

The corrugated fairways of the 13th and 15th can be difficult to find and hold, the 17th is particularly tough in any sort of wind, and the 18th green is not one to overshoot, with the indignity of out-of-bounds immediately beyond the putting surface.

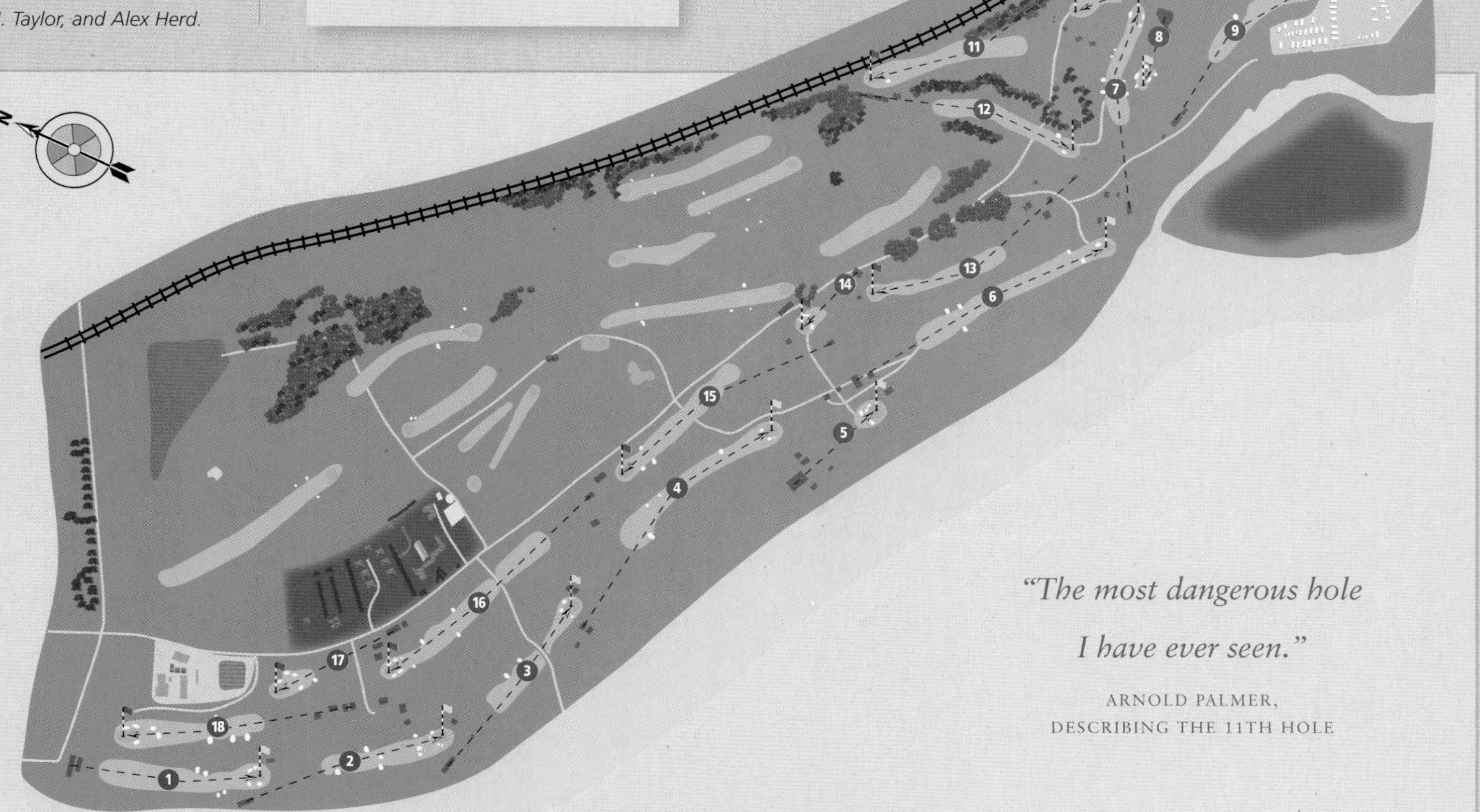

"The most dangerous hole I have ever seen."

ARNOLD PALMER, DESCRIBING THE 11TH HOLE

10

Turnberry

Turnberry

Ailsa Course, Westin Turnberry Hotel, Turnberry, Ayrshire, Scotland

Turnberry's Ailsa Course enjoys the most spectacular setting of the half-dozen courses on the British Open roster. Often compared to California's Pebble Beach, it made its Open debut in 1977 and immediately produced a classic. Yet twice in its history this most majestic of courses was on the brink of extinction.

The railroads played an important part in the spread of golf throughout Britain (America, too, for that matter). They were also responsible for the establishment of some of the country's finest hotels, not least Gleneagles, Cruden Bay, and Turnberry. It was in the early 1900s that the Glasgow and South Western Railway negotiated a lease with the Marquis of Ailsa to enable them to construct a hotel at Turnberry. Already in existence on site was the Marquis's private 13-hole course, and a further 13 holes were added so that by 1906 Turnberry could, with justification, call itself a golf resort. It was good enough to host the British Ladies' Championship of 1912, and a promising future seemed certain.

Unfortunately progress was halted by World War I, when the course became an airfield. After that war restoration was undertaken and the thread of development resumed. Worse destruction came in 1939 in the form of a major air base, a vital part of the defense of transatlantic shipping lanes. Surely that was the end for Turnberry.

NAMING OF HOLES

In common with many Scottish courses, Turnberry's holes are named as well as numbered. The 2nd, for instance, is Mak Siccar ("make sure"), the 3rd Blaw Wearie ("out of breath"), 6th Tappie Tourie ("hit to the top"), 10th Dinna Fouter ("don't mess about"), 13th Tickly Tap ("a tricky little hit"), 15th Ca Canny ("take care"), 17th Lang Whang ("good whack").

LEFT *The short 11th, with the lighthouse and Ailsa Craig—the very essence of golf at Turnberry, a scene far removed from the runways of a wartime airfield.*

▶ In the final round of the 1979 European Open, played at Turnberry, Sandy Lyle birdied six of the first seven holes to establish an eight-shot lead, going on to win the tournament comfortably. The one hole he failed to birdie was the comparatively simple 2nd.

A remarkable resurrection

It was not the end, however, in the mind of Turnberry's manager, Frank Hole. Despite huge obstacles he managed to garner sufficient compensation from public funds after World War II and enough support from the newly formed British Railways, the hotel's owners, to turn three concrete runways and all their attendant paraphernalia into a golf course worthy of the site. What Scottish designer Philip Mackenzie Ross produced was one of the most visually attractive courses in Scotland.

Turnberry then worked its way up the tournament ladder and in 1977 it got its just reward—its first British Open. It turned out to be one of the greatest of all, the famous "duel in the sun," with Tom Watson and Jack Nicklaus going head-to-head to produce some of the most spectacular golf ever seen, Watson just managing to hold out the battling Nicklaus in a thrilling contest.

It could be argued that the first three holes of the Ailsa Course sail under the radar a little, because the player is already anticipating the stretch of shoreline holes from the 4th to the 11th, unparalleled on British Open courses and worthy of comparison with those famed seaside holes at Pebble Beach. The seascapes are stunning, especially at sunset, but the golf requires full concentration, with a number of holes threaded down valleys between the dunes, others (such as the short 4th and 6th holes) fully exposed to the wind on top of the dunes. Arguably, the curving 8th is the best of these demanding par 4s, but the visitor cannot wait to be photographed on the peninsular 9th tee, the drive being made over sufficient of the ocean toward a distant clifftop fairway to cause trepidation in many an otherwise proficient player.

Perhaps the austerities of postwar Britain suggested to Ross a minimalist approach to bunkering, but this aspect was tightened in preparation for the 2009 British Open, Turnberry's fourth. The second course, renamed Kintyre, has also been almost wholly remodeled by Donald Steel.

CARD OF THE COURSE

Hole	*Distance (yards)*	*Par*
1	350	4
2	430	4
3	462	4
4	165	3
5	442	4
6	231	3
7	529	5
8	431	4
9	454	4
Out	3,494	35
10	452	4
11	174	3
12	446	4
13	412	4
14	449	4
15	209	3
16	409	4
17	497	5
18	434	4
In	3,482	35
Total	**6,976**	**70**

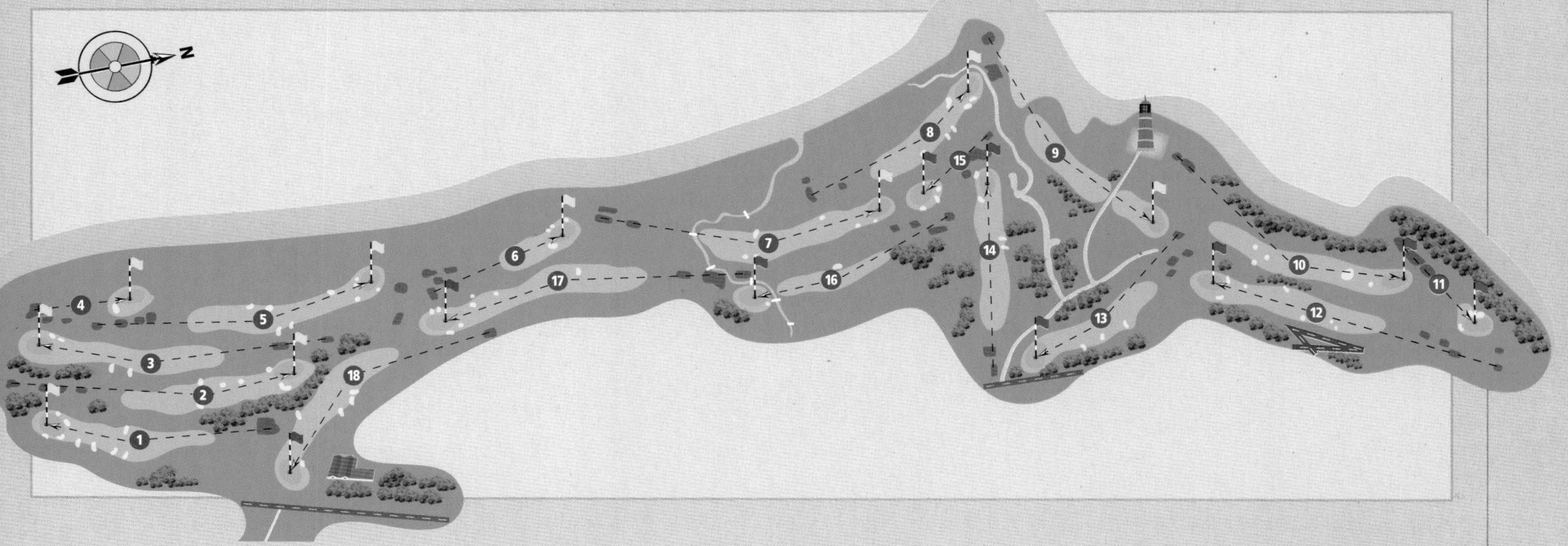

The Belfry

The Belfry

Brabazon Course, The Belfry, Warwickshire, England

The Brabazon boasts a unique record—it is the only course on either side of the Atlantic to have hosted four Ryder Cups, with the Europeans winning in 1985 and 2002, the Americans winning in 1993, and the 1989 match halved. It has, then, been a happy hunting ground for the Europeans.

Driving past the courses (there are three) today, all you can see is a fairly unpromising, flat site with lines of parallel trees indicating where fairways might be located. Had you driven past before the courses were built you would not even have seen the trees, for these were potato fields on cold Midlands clay. The property had none of the qualities you would normally look for in assessing its suitability for golf, and golf of the highest class at that.

The job of creating a silk purse out of a sow's ear fell to Peter Alliss and Dave Thomas, and Thomas has returned over the years to make changes and tweaks to allow the course to keep pace with the prodigious advances in performance of golfers, golf clubs and golf balls, particularly over the past twenty years. Alliss and Thomas created a workmanlike course of good length and plenty of challenge on a remarkably modest acreage.

BELOW *The tough 473-yard/ 433-m par-4 18th on the Brabazon Course at the Belfry, one of golf's finest finishing holes, involving two nail-biting crossings of the lake.*

For most of us the strategy of the Brabazon is about avoiding coming to grief in the many streams and lakes that enter into play on almost every hole. There is some prolific bunkering, too, not least on the short 7th, which, from the tee, suggests something out of Pine Valley. Card-wrecking holes come as early as the 3rd, a reachable par 5 (particularly from the everyday tees) with a corner of a lake to be carried on the way to the green, and we might even fall into the pond on the short 12th simply because it is there. But the holes that expose us all (amateur hacker and world star alike) are the 10th and 18th.

Two world-class holes

The 10th is a very short par 4, which actually gets better the shorter it is played. For the Ryder Cup it is reduced from its full 311 yards/284 m to around 270 yards/247 m. The reason is simple: to tempt the contestants to go for the green from the tee. You could get there with two 9-irons. But what would you not give for a putt for an eagle two? Get it wrong, of course, and you are fishing your ball out of the water or you have bounced off the branches of the green-side trees into perdition.

Perhaps the best is kept for last. This is one of the scariest drives in golf, those needing to attack the hole having to clear as much of the lake on the left as they dare. If that is successful, the second shot is played uphill over a further stretch of lake to an enormously long, three-tiered green. All golfers should play this hole once in their lives if only to understand the courage of those Ryder Cup players who have made par or birdie here under monumental pressure.

RIGHT *The attractive 10th, a siren hole, luring most golfers into an attempt to drive the green, with the capacity to force most of them to reload—three off the tee!*

CARD OF THE COURSE

Hole	Distance (yards)	Par	Hole	Distance (yards)	Par
1	411	4	10	311	4
2	379	4	11	419	4
3	538	5	12	208	3
4	442	4	13	384	4
5	408	4	14	190	3
6	395	4	15	545	5
7	177	3	16	413	4
8	428	4	17	564	5
9	433	4	18	473	4
Out	3,611	36	In	3,507	36
			Total	7,118	72

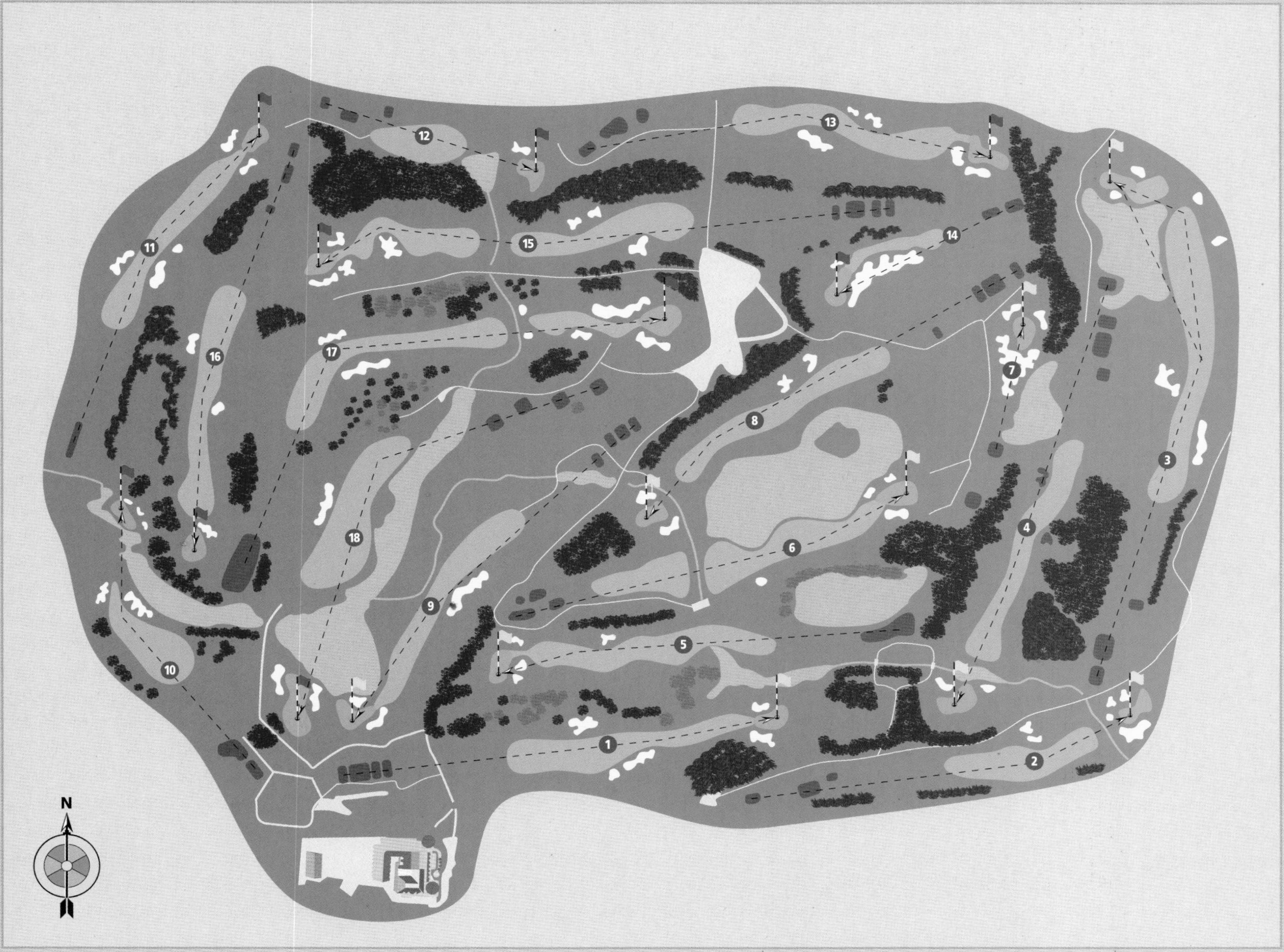

12

Ganton

Ganton

Ganton Golf Club, Scarborough, North Yorkshire, England

If you had to choose a single golf course to encapsulate all that's good about English golf, Ganton would be as good a choice as any. It's old, founded in 1891; it has hosted many high quality tournaments, amateur and professional; it's a mix of heathland and links golf; it's a traditional club yet warmly hospitable; and it's also a great test of all departments of a player's game.

Driving to the course along the busy York–Scarborough road, you could be forgiven for wondering if this were the right road—it just doesn't look like golfing country. Turn down the lane leading to the club and everything changes, even the quality of the air! There are tantalizing glimpses of immaculate fairways and greens, tall pines, cavernous bunkers, and hostile gorse. Already it is apparent that only the A game will do.

Ganton is a compact course, which helps to ensure that the pace of play is brisk, although the ingenious routing brings golfers together at different stages of their rounds. Ganton members are sociable, taking every opportunity to compare notes on their respective matches.

INLAND LINKS

What sets the course at Ganton apart from its immediate surroundings is the land on which it was built. This used to be the beach, many thousands of years ago, before the sea retreated to where it is today. Beneath the course is a deep layer of sand giving excellent drainage and supporting the sort of crisp turf more usually encountered at the seaside. Ganton plays like a links, firm and fast. The pitch-and-run shot is usually far more effective than the high-hit wedge, especially in a strong wind, funneled through the Vale of Pickering.

RIGHT *Ganton's 14th is one of the finest par 4s under 300 yards/274 m in Britain. The setting, in the Vale of Pickering, makes Ganton one of the loveliest places to play.*

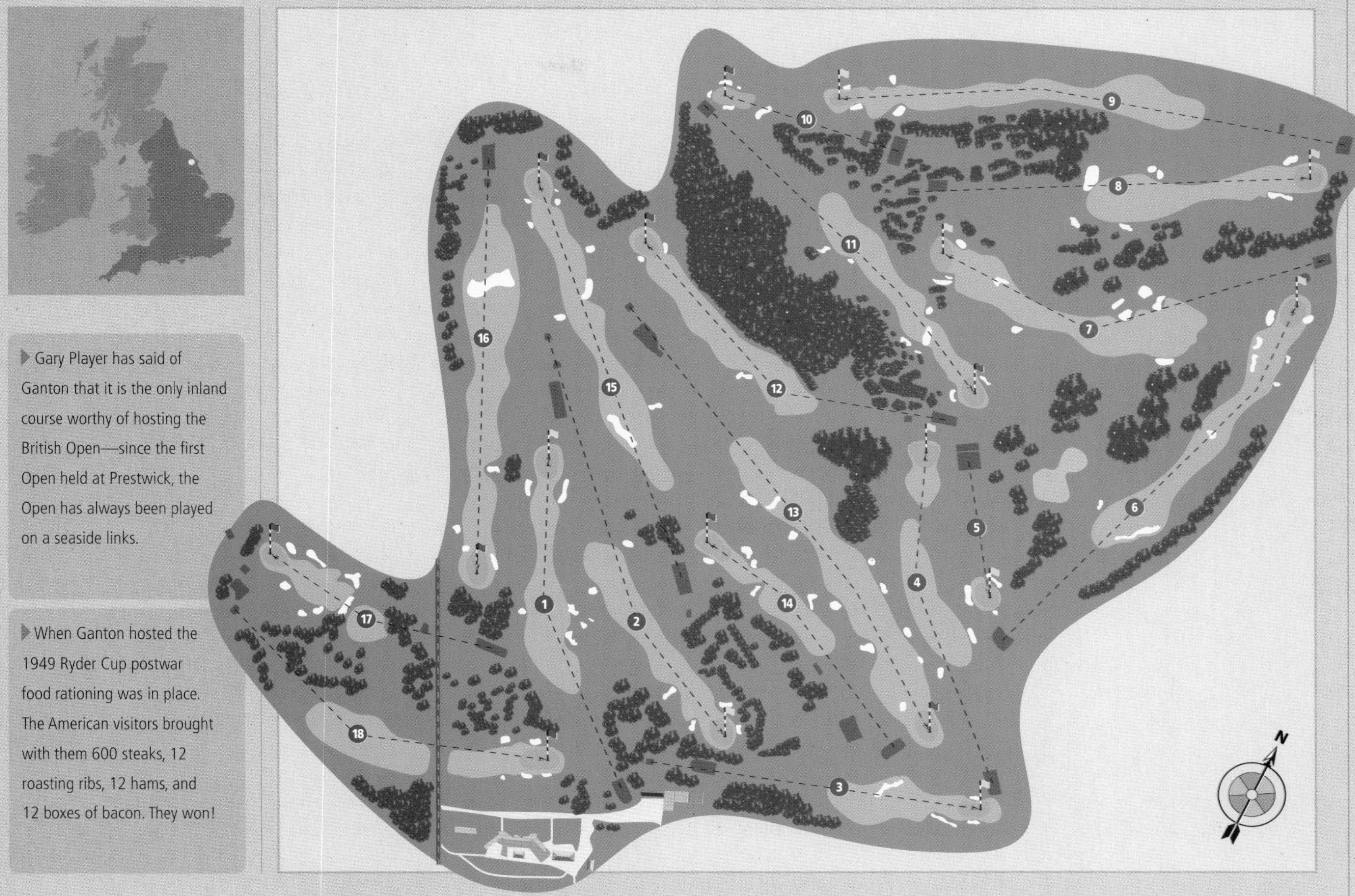

Gary Player has said of Ganton that it is the only inland course worthy of hosting the British Open—since the first Open held at Prestwick, the Open has always been played on a seaside links.

When Ganton hosted the 1949 Ryder Cup postwar food rationing was in place. The American visitors brought with them 600 steaks, 12 roasting ribs, 12 hams, and 12 boxes of bacon. They won!

On the course

The prospect from the 1st tee is inviting, a welcoming fairway rising gently in front of you, before sliding to the right past bunkers to a green, bunkered on either side of the entrance. It is not a difficult hole, but you are immediately aware that sloppy play will not go unpunished. Again, it is the bunkering that keeps you on your toes on the 2nd, and bunkering provides a stiff challenge for those aspiring to drive the 3rd green. From here the course twists and turns over a sequence of delightful holes, meeting the wind from every angle, until on the 14th the course bares its teeth. It may be a short par 4, but it is a brilliant one, tempting bold play and cruelly punishing the inadequate.

Strong hitting is needed to conquer the 15th, and it will be useful on the 16th tee where you are required to clear a monumental quarry of a bunker in mid-fairway. The harder task is positioning the drive correctly to grant an unimpeded approach to the green, raised above bunkers and backed by bright yellow gorse. The 17th is a brutal long short hole (played as a par 4 by visitors), and the round ends with a supremely strategic dogleg. Greed will bring disaster! Then it's time for a drink and a slice of the famous Ganton cake.

CARD OF THE COURSE

Hole	*Distance (yards)*	*Par*	*Hole*	*Distance (yards)*	*Par*
1	373	4	10	168	3
2	445	4	11	417	4
3	334	4	12	363	4
4	406	4	13	524	5
5	157	3	14	282	4
6	470	4	15	461	4
7	435	4	16	448	4
8	414	4	17	249	3
9	504	5	18	434	4
Out	3,538	36	In	3,346	35
			Total	**6,884**	**71**

Royal Birkdale

Royal Birkdale

Royal Birkdale Golf Club, Southport, Merseyside, England

There is refreshingly little pomp for a club and course with such history. The respect of being chosen for the 100th British Open and a consistent ranking in the U.K. Top 10 are quite sufficient for Royal Birkdale.

A striking sight greets visitors to Royal Birkdale: a white art-deco clubhouse resembling a ship sailing on a tossing sea of sand dunes. It was designed in 1935 to replicate the superstructure of the ocean liners that in those days steamed out from Liverpool in considerable numbers, heading for all corners of the then intact British Empire. Within the clubhouse, however, its creature comforts most definitely belong to the 21st century.

True links golf is played in partnership with nature, and Birkdale's course uses little trickery or human intervention to create its challenges, the difficulties coming instead with subtle design and substantial yardages. Thick rough and willow scrub devour errant shots, and act as a wonderful haven for a wide variety of wildlife. However, the design (evolved over the years by the Hawtree family of golf course architects) is actually very simple: holes weave through valleys between sand hills, creating flat fairways (for a links!) giving the reward of many yards of roll on a well-struck shot, and a good stance for the next shot. The crests and troughs of that tossing sea of sand dunes are omnipresent, but you are only troubled by them if you stray off line. There are some fine tee and green sites high on them, such as the 11th tee and 12th green.

A long and distinguished championship history

Host to the British Open on nine occasions between 1954 and 2008, Royal Birkdale always proves to be an outstanding venue, with its fair nature rewarding good play, while the sand hills lining the fairways create a set of natural grandstands for spectators, the best of any course on the Open roster. The overriding feedback from every Open is that the course is hard but fair, and it is a consistent favorite with the professionals.

▶ The rough can be brutal for Open week. In 1971 Lee Trevino joked: ". . . at 15 we put down my bag to hunt for a ball, found the ball, lost the bag!"

LEFT *Overlooking the final green, Royal Birkdale's unique clubhouse resembles an ocean liner, so many of which used to steam past the course on their way out from Liverpool.*

The difficult 1st, a long, left-hand dogleg, sets the precedent that accurate hitting is key, with out-of-bounds right, the infamous "Jutland" bunker on the left, and characteristic mounds that block approaches to the green from poor positions. Although trees are never a factor in regulation play, they often provide a handsome backdrop, such as when they top the dunes behind the 2nd green, a green cunningly contoured and guarded by pot bunkers.

As with all good designs, planning from the tee is essential to allow the correct approach shot to the green, such as on the tough 6th, on which one must flirt with a huge bunker on the right to leave a decent angle to the elevated green. The holes twist and turn through the dunes allowing the prevailing wind to hit from every angle.

There is good variation to the holes, with short par 4s such as the dogleg 5th and downhill 11th both requiring good management. The greens, which were completely rebuilt by Martin Hawtree in the 1990s, are a fine test, with mounds, hollows, and clever bunkering around them calling for an imaginative short game, summed up by Seve Ballesteros's famous chip-and-run between the bunkers on the 18th in 1976.

A PROUD MOMENT FOR GOLF

One of golf's great gentlemen, Jack Nicklaus generously conceded a short but missable putt to Tony Jacklin on the 18th green at the climax of the 1969 Ryder Cup at Birkdale, a putt that allowed the home team to tie with the Americans. "I am sure you would have holed, but I was not prepared to see you miss," was Nicklaus's brotherly remark to his opponent.

CARD OF THE COURSE

Hole	Distance (yards)	Par
1	449	4
2	421	4
3	407	4
4	203	3
5	344	4
6	480	4
7	177	3
8	457	4
9	411	4
Out	3,349	34
10	403	4
11	408	4
12	183	3
13	498	4
14	198	3
15	544	5
16	416	4
17	547	5
18	472	4
In	3,669	36
Total	7,018	70

Royal Liverpool

Royal Liverpool Golf Club, Hoylake, Wirral, England

Founded in 1869, Royal Liverpool (or Hoylake as it is popularly known) is one of England's oldest golf clubs. Golf was first played here alongside amateur horse and pony races, for this was the site of the Liverpool Hunt Club. Naturally, the horses were not expected to charge up and down the sand dunes, so, for the most part, this is an unusually flat course. But appearances can be deceptive, especially here.

In no time at all (1872) Hoylake had attracted its first professional tournament—in fact the first of any significance outside Scotland. The first prize was almost double the prize for the British Open. It attracted a small but distinguished field with Young Tom Morris emerging victorious. Next up was the inaugural Amateur Championship (1885), followed by its first British Open (1897). The winner on this occasion was Royal Liverpool's own Harold Hilton; he and his club companion John Ball were the only amateurs to win the British Open until the emergence of Bob Jones, who won at Hoylake in 1930. This was to become the second leg of his incredible "Impregnable Quadrilateral," when he won the Open and Amateur Championships of the United States and Britain in the same year.

The Open returned to Hoylake several times, but after Roberto de Vicenzo's victory in 1967 there was a lengthy gap until 2006, when Tiger Woods showed everybody else how to play the course.

RIGHT *The 12th green presents a difficult target, raised up on top of the dunes, but it gives wonderful views over the Dee Estuary to the Flintshire hills.*

Woods—the great strategist

As he had done previously at St. Andrews in 2005, Woods analyzed the course from the point of view of his own strengths, deciding that it was too dangerous to use the driver prospectively from the tee. He reckoned that if he played for position rather than length, making sure that his tee shot landed in the best spot from which to approach the green, his long-iron play to the green would get him close to the hole. His approach play that week was imperious.

The order of the holes was altered for the Open, but more usually Hoylake begins with a unique hole, a bunkerless par 4 on which it is possible to drive out of bounds on either side. The green adjoins a "cop" (a grassy bank, typical of Hoylake) which is also out of bounds. Like the first hole, most of the early holes are level, but there is a relentlessness about the probing that never lets up. The wind rarely lets up either.

As the round progresses the character of the course changes gradually until the 8th, when the pitch is made steeply uphill to a rolling green standing on top of the dunes, giving way to a glorious sequence of seaside holes with expansive views. The pick of these must be the 12th, a majestic par 4 beginning with a drive to a low, curving fairway, followed by a long second shot uphill to a brilliantly sited green, repelling all but the finest approaches. Woods solved its problems on the second day of the Open by pitching in for an eagle. His approach, stone dead, on the final afternoon was breathtaking. Great golf on a great course!

▶ For the 2006 Open a number of alterations were made to the course, including a brand new 17th hole (played as the 1st for the championship). The old green was so near to a road that it was not unknown for players to putt out of bounds.

CARD OF THE COURSE

Hole	*Distance (yards)*	*Par*
1	429	4
2	372	4
3	528	5
4	202	3
5	453	4
6	423	4
7	198	3
8	534	5
9	393	4
Out	3,532	36
10	448	4
11	198	3
12	456	4
13	161	3
14	554	5
15	459	4
16	560	5
17	454	4
18	436	4
In	3,726	36
Total	**7,258**	**72**

"I know no better golf course anywhere in the world."

BERNARD DARWIN

▶ The 6th hole is unusual among championship courses in that the drive is made over the corner of an orchard.

Royal Lytham

Royal Lytham

Royal Lytham and St. Annes Golf Club, Lancashire, England

English golf is full of surprises, and one of those surprises has to be Royal Lytham. It lies on a somewhat unprepossessing chunk of land, the Fylde, whose crowning glory is the rather dowdy holiday resort of Blackpool. Hopes are not raised by the immediate surroundings of the club, with neither a sand dune to be seen nor a breaking wave. In fact the club is enclosed by housing and a railroad track. Yet there is no denying that this is one of England's great clubs with one of its finest courses, well worthy of its frequent hosting of the British Open.

Lytham made an auspicious start to its Open career. The year was 1926 and the winner was none other than Bob Jones, the greatest amateur golfer the game has known. No further Opens were held there until after World War II when an illustrious list of champions was produced: Bobby Locke, Peter Thomson, Bob Charles, Tony Jacklin, Gary Player, and Seve Ballesteros (twice). Yet there were no Americans in that group. Amends were made in 1996, 70 years after that first American triumph, when Tom Lehman emerged as champion, reinforced in 2001 when David Duval realized the full potential of his talent.

Each one of those great champions needed abundant grit and determination, for Lytham never lets up. It is a very well-defended course and utterly unforgiving.

EUROPE'S RESURGENCE

When Tony Jacklin won the Open at Lytham in 1969 it proved to be an influential moment in British and European golf, because it signaled the start of a resurgence in self-belief. No longer did the Europeans fear the Americans, Australians, and South Africans who previously had dominated world golf. It paved the way for wins in majors by Sandy Lyle, Ian Woosnam, Seve Ballesteros, Bernhard Langer, José María Olazábal, Nick Faldo, Paul Lawrie, and Padraig Harrington.

Nothing is orthodox at Lytham

That is not to say that Lytham is eccentric—far from it! But it is unusual in opening with a par 3, and to have three par 4s well under 400 yards/366 m on the back nine is far from today's norm. Yet that back nine is fearsome. Scores are made on the way out, more often than not lost on the way home.

Lytham is relentless. For the average player it is probably the most examining of all the Open tests, largely because of its prolific bunkering. As British Open has succeeded British Open and equipment has developed and player prowess grown, new bunkers have had to be added each time in order to stiffen the challenge. The old ones have been left intact. They threaten shots of every length on each hole.

It is an educative experience following great players over the closing holes. Of the 15th hole Jack Nicklaus once exclaimed, "God! It's a hard hole!" The fairway is angled across the line of the drive, narrow and well bunkered. A conservative drive leaves a blind shot, against the wind, to find the green. In 1979 Seve Ballesteros played an amazing recovery shot from a car park to the right of the 16th green for an unlikely birdie on his way to winning the championship. For the rest of us the best approach is from the left.

Bob Jones made an astonishing recovery on the 17th on his final round in 1926, so remarkable a shot that a plaque is set in the ground to the left of the fairway bunkers to commemorate it. With two diagonal lines of bunkers crossing the fairway, the final drive is one of the more nerve-racking in golf, and many a championship has been thrown away on this hole.

LEFT *The clubhouse was built by Woolfall and Eccles of Liverpool, who had recently completed the Royal Liverpool clubhouse. It was to be "a picturesque building, with the introduction of half-timbering."*

CARD OF THE COURSE

Hole	Distance (yards)	Par
1	206	3
2	438	4
3	458	4
4	392	4
5	212	3
6	494	5
7	557	5
8	419	4
9	164	3
Out	3,340	35
10	335	4
11	542	5
12	198	3
13	342	4
14	445	4
15	465	4
16	359	4
17	467	4
18	412	4
In	3,565	36
Total	6,905	71

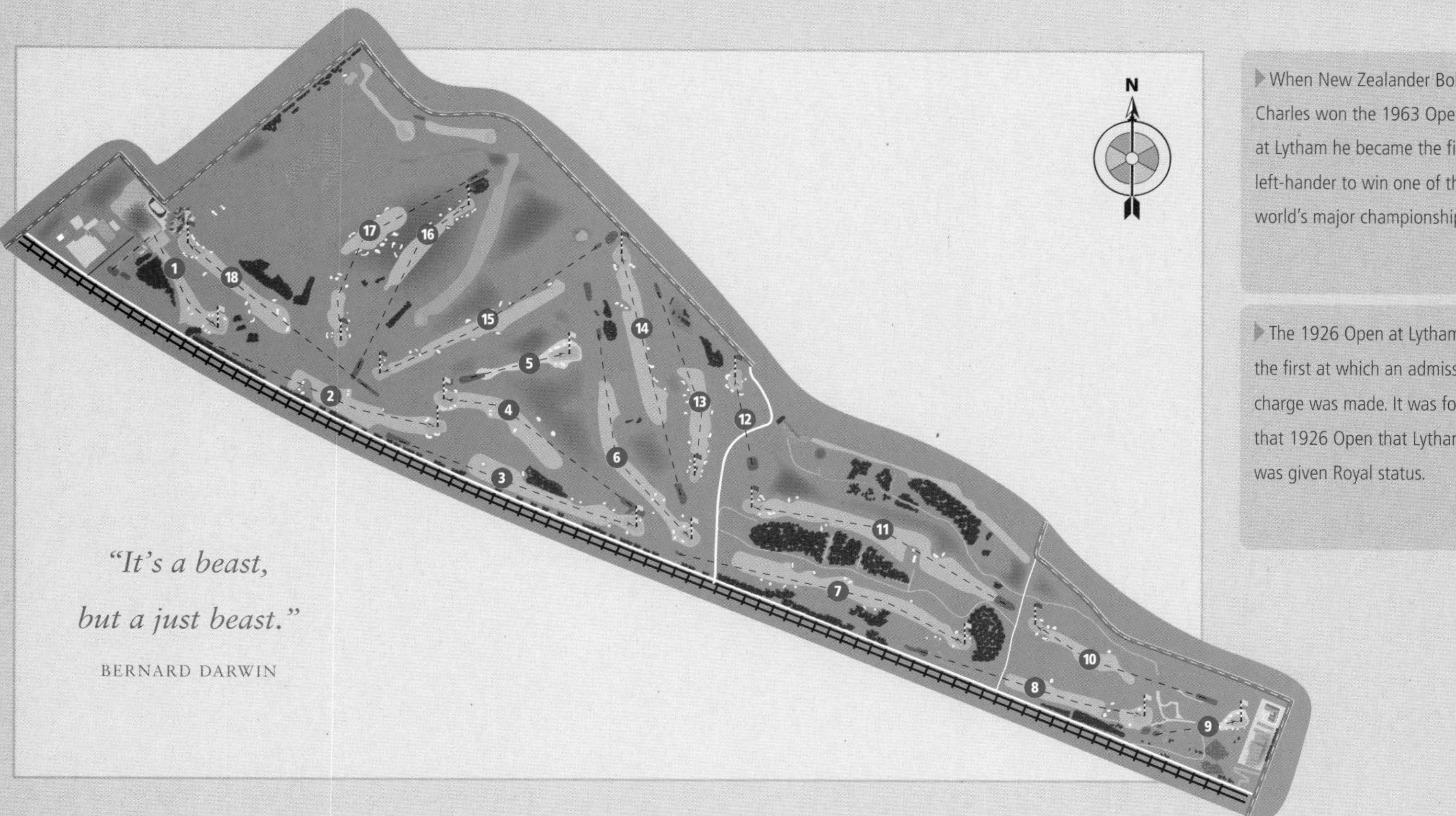

When New Zealander Bob Charles won the 1963 Open at Lytham he became the first left-hander to win one of the world's major championships.

The 1926 Open at Lytham was the first at which an admission charge was made. It was for that 1926 Open that Lytham was given Royal status.

"It's a beast, but a just beast."

BERNARD DARWIN

Royal St. George's

Royal St. George's

Royal St. George's Golf Club, Sandwich, Kent, England

The British Open was a Scottish monopoly for the first 33 years of its existence, but in 1894 the championship was allowed to be played south of Hadrian's Wall for the very first time. It could hardly have ventured much farther south, for it came to the Kent coast at Sandwich, where the Royal St. George's Golf Club had been established (by two Scotsmen, of course) in 1887.

Our two Scotsmen (Dr. Laidlaw Purves and Henry Lamb) had traveled along much of England's Channel coast in an attempt to find a piece of ground that resembled those of the great links of their native land. They were beginning to despair of ever discovering what they were searching for, when—at Sandwich—they found a wild, tumbling wilderness in which an exciting and exceedingly challenging course could be built.

A natural course

On such land, Purves and Lamb had no need to engage in lengthy earthmoving. It was merely a matter of finding as varied a routing out and back as they could through, across, and along the dunes. They did such a good job that the course follows much the same route today. There have been changes, though, not least the elimination of blind shots and one particularly blind par 3—the Maiden.

RIGHT *The 6th green, right in the heart of some of the finest duneland on earth. Farther along the shore lies Prince's Golf Club, host to the 1932 British Open.*

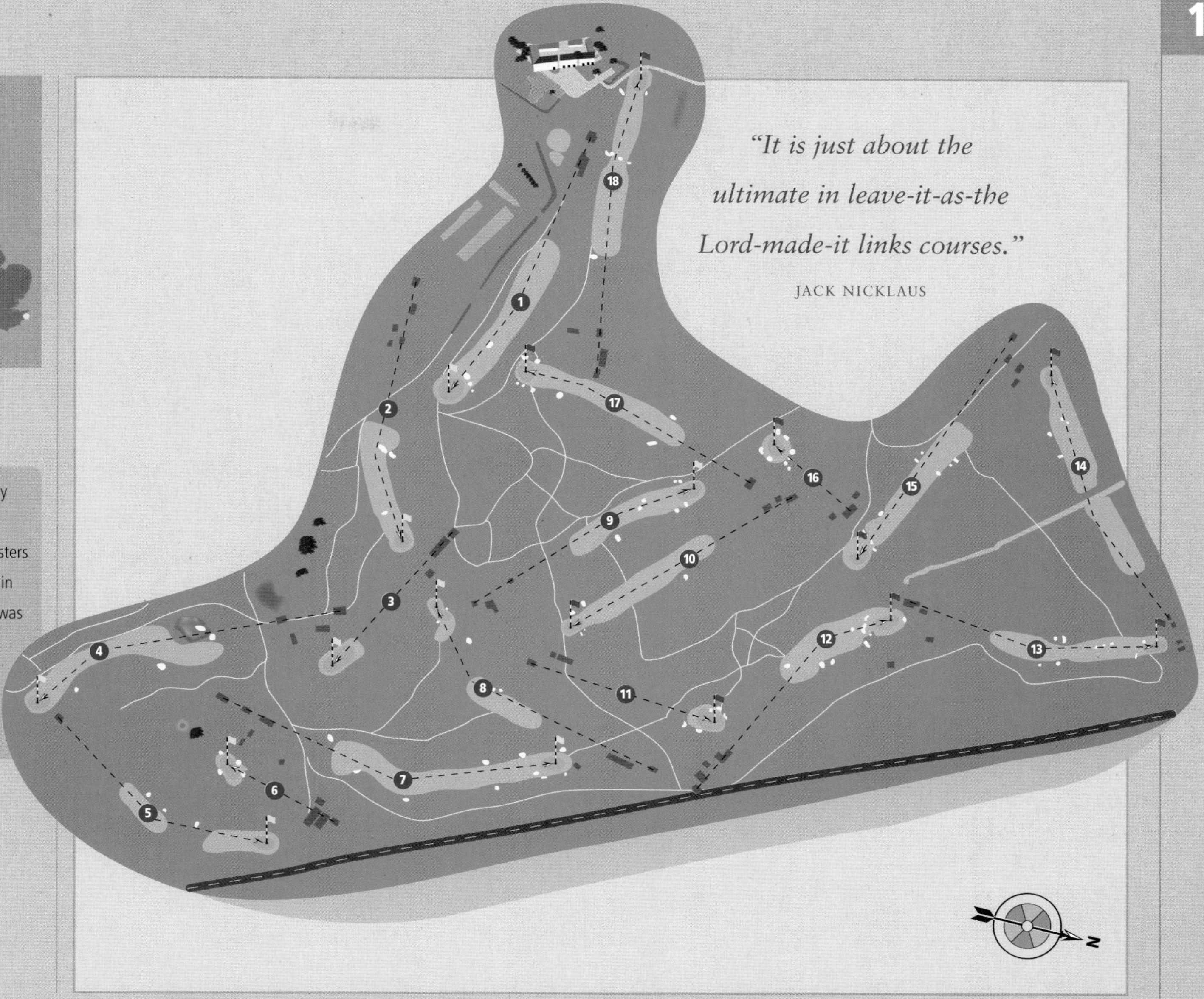

▶ A little bit of golfing history was made on the 16th hole during the 1967 Dunlop Masters tournament when Tony Jacklin holed his tee shot in one: it was the first time an ace had been broadcast live on British television.

"It is just about the ultimate in leave-it-as-the Lord-made-it links courses."

JACK NICKLAUS

CARD OF THE COURSE

Hole	Distance (yards)	Par	Hole	Distance (yards)	Par
1	441	4	10	413	4
2	413	4	11	240	3
3	210	3	12	380	4
4	494	4	13	459	4
5	421	4	14	551	5
6	172	3	15	478	4
7	530	5	16	163	3
8	455	4	17	425	4
9	389	4	18	468	4
Out	3,525	35	In	3,577	35
			Total	7,102	70

Of all the British Open courses it is Sandwich that feels the most removed from everyday life, the clubhouse sitting as it were in the fields at the end of a track. And that sense of remoteness continues on the opening hole, striking out into the wide expanses, long and far. On the 4th the first-time visitor might be somewhat perplexed at the prospect from the tee, for a giant sand dune bars the way to the distant fairway, and in its face are set two of the most fearsome bunkers imaginable. It is the beginning of a wonderful sequence of holes taking play to the sea shore.

There is respite of a kind around the turn, but the run home from the 14th is the stuff of white knuckles. Indeed, that 14th has ruined many an Open aspirant's chances, with an out-of-bounds wall keeping worryingly close company with the fairway all the way to the green. (Prince's Golf Club, venue for the 1932 British Open, won by Gene Sarazen, lies on the other side of that wall.) Sturdy hitting is required to surmount the difficulties of the three remaining long two-shot holes, very exposed to the wind as they are, yet the delicate 16th is no pushover, despite its being the shortest hole on the course.

17

Sunningdale

Sunningdale

Old Course, Sunningdale Golf Club, Berkshire, England

Membership of Sunningdale Golf Club is one of the most sought after in England. First and foremost it is a true members' club, with a wonderful spirit and atmosphere to be found in the clubhouse and on the course. Additionally, Sunningdale is one of those few privileged clubs to possess two equally great courses, the Old and the New. Having been at the forefront of English golf for over a century there is also a great sense of tradition and history.

When golf was first introduced to England in 1608, the game was played on the short, links-like grasses of Blackheath. Scots had brought the game with them when they traveled south with their recently crowned king, James I of England, James VI of Scotland. Hardly surprisingly, they sought the nearest thing they could find to linksland on which to play their golf. Having found Blackheath they did not need to look elsewhere. They had no cause to travel into the county of Surrey, which was then heavily forested with few towns, so they never discovered the golfing potential that awaited some 20 miles/32 km from the center of London.

In fact it was not until the last two decades of the 19th century that golf took root in this part of England, assisted in no small part by the coming of the railroads and the invention of commuting. The mainly professional people who moved into the country from London—the doctors, lawyers, bankers, and stockbrokers—began to establish golf clubs where they lived. To their delight they found that the land here, on a sandbelt stretching from Berkshire through Surrey to Hampshire and West Sussex, could provide them with ideal ground for firm and fast golf, a world away from golfing on the damp and heavy clays of London.

THE PERFECT ROUND

Qualifying rounds for the British Open in 1926 were held at Sunningdale, where Bob Jones recorded a 66 and a 68—a performance described by Bernard Darwin as "incredible and indecent." His 66 (33 out, 33 in) included 33 putts and 33 other shots, and each hole was a three or a four. It was described at the time as the finest round of golf ever shot in Britain.

LEFT *The par-5 10th, one of the most handsome holes on a notably attractive course. Park and Colt used the topography of Sunningdale admirably.*

Sunningdale leads the way

Although there were already a number of established golf courses in the area, Sunningdale set a new standard when it opened for play in 1901, and from the start the whole venture was heavily publicized. The course was designed by the former British Open champion, Willie Park Jr., and he sought to reproduce the features of links golf that had, so far, been largely missing from inland golf in England. Golfers were required to think in a very different way, to plot their way round a series of subtle, not coarse, challenges.

CARD OF THE COURSE

Hole	Distance (yards)	Par	Hole	Distance (yards)	Par
1	494	5	10	478	5
2	489	5	11	325	4
3	319	4	12	451	4
4	161	3	13	185	3
5	419	4	14	509	5
6	415	4	15	226	3
7	402	4	16	438	4
8	182	3	17	421	4
9	273	4	18	432	4
Out	3,154	36	In	3,465	36
			Total	**6,619**	**72**

BELOW RIGHT *The 17th hole, and beyond it the 18th, leading to Sunningdale's fine clubhouse. These two strong par 4s provide the climax of an excellent finish.*

Park was perhaps unlucky in that his design work coincided with the demise of the old guttie ball and the arrival of the new Haskell ball with its increased performance. The club, however, was far from unlucky in having appointed Harry Colt as its inaugural secretary. He it was who rebuilt the course in the 1920s into what we know today, adding the equally good New Course at the same time.

Playing Sunningdale Old Course is a complete experience, with a magical routing making superb use of every natural feature available to the architect to give the golfer pause for thought. These are not greens to be blitzed with lob wedges. Rather, the ball needs to be caressed into and on to the putting surface. There are holes of all lengths and sizes, giving great change of pace and requiring wisdom on every tee, for drive in the wrong area and there is little hope of stopping the next shot on the green. As you would expect at such a club, both Sunningdale courses are always presented in perfect condition.

Wentworth

West Course, Wentworth Club, Virginia Water, Surrey, England

Driving through the vast Wentworth Estate is a voyage of discovery. The mansions of the rich and famous line the lanes and drives, many of them backing on to the fairways of the three golf courses that occasionally cross the roads, causing the driver to stop while a four-ball launches its tee shots on their journeys.

ABOVE *Wentworth's West Course is as visually attractive as it is demanding. It is one of those courses that invites you to play good shots. This is the par-3 2nd.*

The Wentworth Estate came into being in the 1920s through the vision, entrepreneurial skills and extraordinary confidence of a developer—George Tarrant. When it came to constructing the golf courses, Tarrant knew exactly who to use—Harry Colt. Colt and Tarrant had collaborated on a similar scheme some years earlier at St, George's Hill, and the success of both ventures has ensured that both are among the most desirable places to live in the whole London area.

Colt built the East Course in 1924. Today it measures only a little over 6,000 yards/5,486 m, but it is a thoroughly entertaining course and was good enough to host a match between the professionals of America and Great Britain and Ireland in 1926, thus paving the way for the Ryder Cup. The East was also the venue for the inaugural Curtis Cup, between women amateur golfers of the United States and Great Britain and Ireland, in 1932. Second up was the West Course, also Colt-designed, of 1926. There was then a gap of over 60 years until the third course, the Edinburgh, opened in 1990. This was designed by John Jacobs in association with Gary Player and Bernard Gallagher.

▶ In addition to the PGA Championship and World Matchplay, the West Course has hosted the Ryder Cup (1953) and the Canada Cup (1956), when Ben Hogan made one of his all-too-rare visits to the U.K., winning the tournament with Sam Snead as partner.

The Burma Road

When it opened, the West Course was found to be long and hard, tough enough for it to be dubbed the Burma Road. Its length is not so fearsome today but the name has stuck and twice a year television audiences get to see it in fine condition, hosting the PGA Championship in the spring and the World Matchplay in the fall. Recent adjustments to the course by Ernie Els (who lives on the estate) have pushed the overall length up from just over 7,000 yards/ 6,400 m to more than 7,300 yards/6,675 m. Visitors playing it from the yellow tees still find it quite long enough at over 6,700 yards/6,125 m.

Length is not everything, however, and some of the best holes are modest on paper. The delightful 154-yard/141-m 2nd, for instance, is played from a high tee across a road to an elusive ledge green. The 6th, 7th, and 8th are each among the shorter par 4s, but their greens are notoriously hard to locate. The short 14th is played uphill to a multi-level green, the hill being steep enough to deceive the eye, and club selection further complicated if there is a wind. Similarly, the 16th regularly sets problems for the professionals under tournament conditions.

A new tee has been found for the 17th, stretching it to a monstrous—and treacherous—610 yards/558 m. It is all too easy to drive out of bounds on the left, so the natural reaction is to err to the right, increasing the length of the hole and very probably resulting in a clinging lie, or even finishing behind a tree. Nor is the green easy to find, on high ground, the fairway constantly curving. The Els-modified 18th is now a particularly strong finishing hole.

CARD OF THE COURSE

Hole	*Distance (yards)*	*Par*
1	473	5
2	154	3
3	465	4
4	552	5
5	212	3
6	418	4
7	396	4
8	401	4
9	452	4
Out	3,523	36
10	184	3
11	416	4
12	531	5
13	470	4
14	179	3
15	490	4
16	383	4
17	610	5
18	538	5
In	3,801	37
Total	**7,324**	**73**

19

Woodhall Spa

Woodhall Spa

Hotchkin Course, Woodhall Spa, Lincolnshire, England

Of all Britain's great courses the Hotchkin Course at Woodhall Spa must be the least known—for the very simple reason that it lies in a remote corner of the country, not really on the way to or from anywhere. Despite its inviting title, Woodhall Spa is little more than a charming village, but it has had a golf course since 1890.

The club had rather a troubled history, and the local landowner, Stafford Vere Hotchkin, repeatedly came to the rescue, first by writing off the club's rent arrears and in 1919 by buying the club. After a succession of moves and different course layouts, the club was lucky enough to possess, by this time, a fine Harry Colt course laid out on a rare tract of sandy heath. But Hotchkin was not merely a financial benefactor, he was also a more than competent golfer and a course designer himself. Between 1919 and his death in 1953 he made a large number of refinements to the design, turning the course into one of England's most demanding. Hotchkin's son Neil continued to run the club after his father's death, which ensured that the design was not tampered with and Hotchkin's ethos maintained. In 1995 he sold the course to the English Golf Union, who made their headquarters there, bringing in Donald Steel to build a second—and utterly different—course (the Bracken), while keeping Hotchkin's course in the manner of which he would have approved.

RIGHT *The bunkering at Woodhall Spa is among the most formidable in Britain. It is deep, steep-faced, and prolific. This is the 5th green, surrounded by sand.*

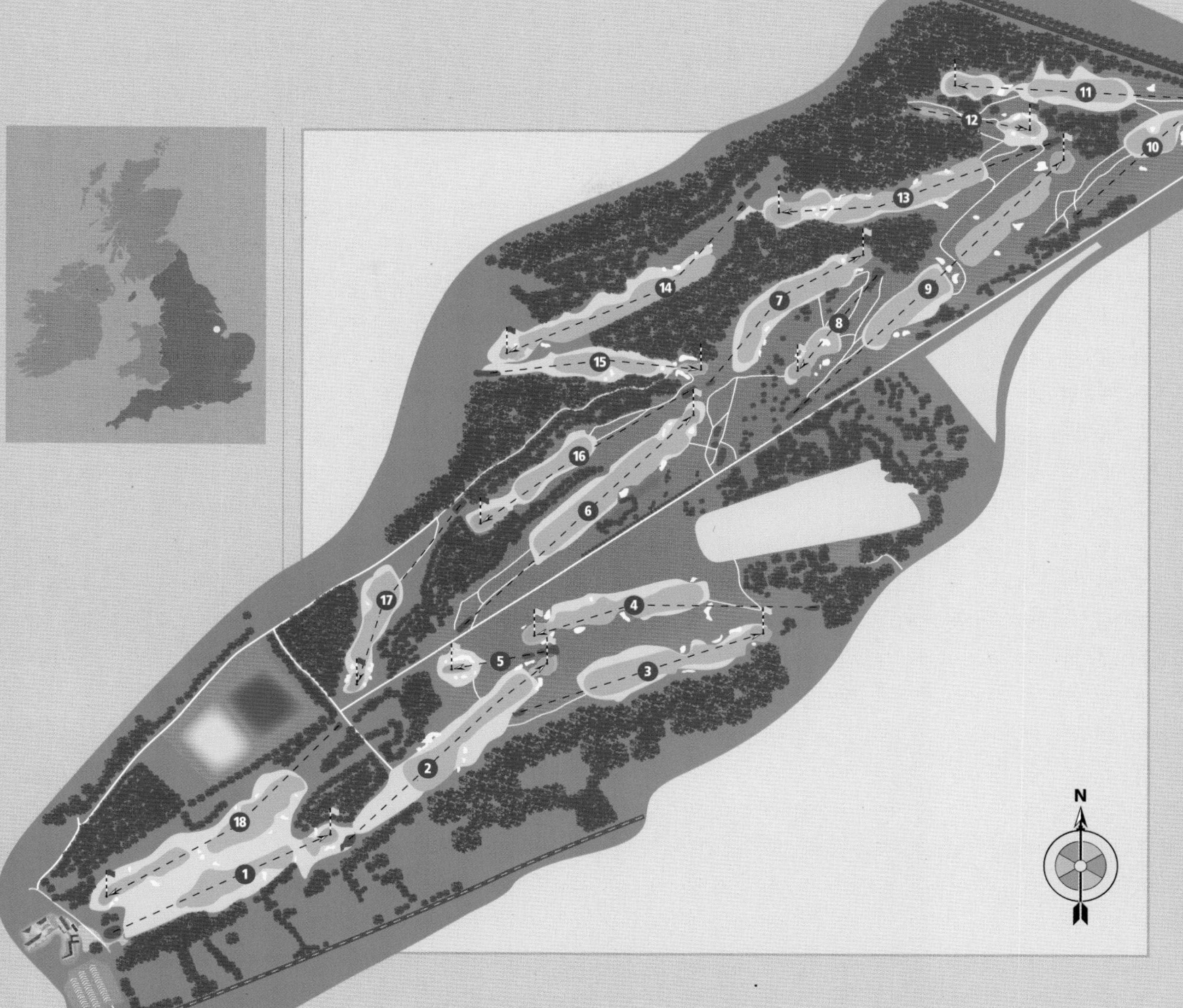

One of Hotchkin's principles of golf course design was: "The best results are obtained by making a course conform to the natural surroundings that already exist, so that it will not look artificial and fail to blend with the landscape." Woodhall Spa is a shining example.

Because of its location Woodhall Spa has staged few professional tournaments, but it has featured prominently in the amateur calendar, hosting such tournaments as the English Amateur, Brabazon Trophy, St. Andrews Trophy, and Ladies' British Open Amateur.

During a club match in 1982 a member holed the 12th in one—as, then, did his opponent, for the half!

CARD OF THE COURSE

Hole	*Distance (yards)*	*Par*	*Hole*	*Distance (yards)*	*Par*
1	361	4	10	338	4
2	442	4	11	437	4
3	415	4	12	172	3
4	414	4	13	451	4
5	148	3	14	521	5
6	526	5	15	321	4
7	470	4	16	395	4
8	209	3	17	336	4
9	584	5	18	540	5
Out	3,569	36	In	3,511	37
			Total	**7,080**	**73**

England's most frightening bunkers?

Until you have played Woodhall Spa it is difficult to imagine just how ferocious its bunkers are. It is a moot point whether Ganton or Woodhall Spa has the most savage bunkering in England. Ganton's are more visible and perhaps more frightening to the eye. Woodhall Spa's bunkers are deeper—sinister trenches very often topped off with eyebrows of heather—and sometimes invisible. A bunker may be as deep as the height of a man. In some cases these are set tight against elevated greens and you may have to raise the ball 10 feet/3 m vertically to gain the safety of the putting surface. The strange thing is that Ganton and Woodhall Spa are such lovely courses that, however roughly they may treat you, you still enjoy the experience immensely.

Woodhall Spa charms you from the outset, with a delicate, short two-shot hole to get play under way. You could be lulled into a false sense of security, but on the 2nd hole the course bares its teeth, with the deepest of bunkers threatening the drive of all lengths of hitters, and the green has a narrow entrance. And if a bunker does not get you the heather most surely will. It may look lovely, but a rash shot out of it may result in a broken wrist.

What makes Woodhall Spa so enticing is the wonderful variety of the holes, with no two the same. There are great long two-shotters, but it may be the collection of par 3s (only three of them) that remain in the memory longest.

IN TUNE WITH NATURE

The Hotchkin Course occupies a valuable piece of heathland, a habitat that is disappearing all too quickly in Britain. It has, therefore, been designated as a Site of Special Scientific Interest. The National Golf Centre works in partnership with Natural England to manage the land to help preserve its biodiversity. It is an ongoing project and will, in time, restore more of the original heathland, removing plants and trees that are not natural to the heath. At the same time, long-lost bunkers and other features from the earlier courses are being discovered and brought back into action.

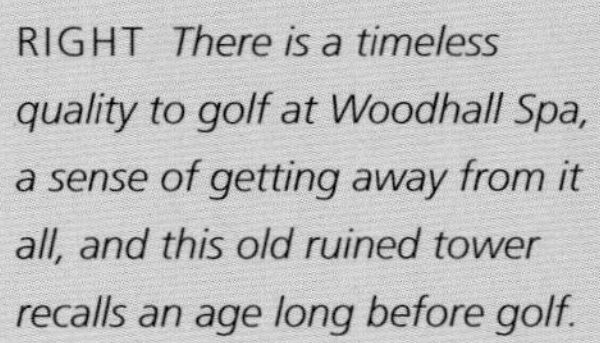

RIGHT *There is a timeless quality to golf at Woodhall Spa, a sense of getting away from it all, and this old ruined tower recalls an age long before golf.*

Celtic Manor

Twenty Ten Course, Celtic Manor Resort, Newport, Wales

The golf courses at Celtic Manor, host to the Ryder Cup in 2010, are contemporary in every way, but the ground over which they run is steeped in ancient history. They overlook the remains of the Roman town of Caerleon and, running from it, the Via Julia was an important communication route connecting this Welsh outpost to the Roman settlements in England. Its remains cross the Celtic Manor estate.

In the 5th century the lands were acquired by the Bishops of Llandaff and in the 17th century a manor house was built for the local high sheriff. But the estate as it now is first took shape in the 1860s when the enormously prosperous industrialist, Thomas Powell, had Coldra House built for his son. Subsequently the house became a maternity hospital. It closed in 1975 and was in danger of falling into ruin until a wealthy businessman, Sir Terry Matthews, bought it in 1981, restoring it for use initially as a small luxury hotel. Since then the story has been one of considerable expansion. The hotel can now accommodate almost 2,000 conference delegates and in 1995 golf arrived on the scene in the shape of the Roman Road Course, which, as its name suggests, keeps close company with the Via Julia.

The Roman Road Course was designed by one of the legends of golf course design, Robert Trent Jones, who in his 70-year career built over 300 courses, including the Ryder Cup venue, Valderrama, in Spain, and made alterations to a further 150. Jones returned to Celtic Manor to build a short course, Coldra Woods, and later to team up with his son, Robert Jr., to lay out the enormously long Wentwood Hills Course—an extraordinary mix of alpine holes and others that might have been lifted bodily from Florida, with the obligatory lakes to the fore in the lowland section.

▶ Thomas Powell, founder of the Powell-Duffryn Company and the world's first millionaire, employed 13,500 workers in his coal business, 11,600 of them working underground.

LEFT *The tranquillity of the Usk Valley will become a cauldron of high emotion when the Ryder Cup matches are played at Celtic Manor. This is the 14th.*

Bold decisions

Matthews was ambitious for his resort. He wanted to attract the biggest stars in the game to play there and he set out to bring the Ryder Cup to Wales for the first time. His problem was that none of his existing courses could accommodate such a tournament. Roman Road was not tough enough and Wentwood Hills was spectator-unfriendly, with an exhausting hill climb required on the back nine. Drastic measures were needed, and Matthews was not afraid to take bold decisions.

The boldest decision was to abandon the Wentwood Hills Course, considered the jewel in the crown of the resort. It has not been wasted, for the upland holes have been incorporated in a new course designed by Colin Montgomerie, and nine of the low-lying holes have been retained as part of the course specifically designed to attract the Ryder Cup, lying entirely in the Usk Valley. Matthews's brave move was successful, and the Ryder Cup matches will be played in Wales for the first time in 2010, on this course now known as the Twenty Ten.

As might be expected, it is a heroic course playing to almost 7,500 yards/ 6,858 m from the back tees. For those matches that make it to the par-5 18th hole—one of three par 5s over 600 yards/549 m—there remains a death-or-glory gamble on whether to try to reach the green in two across a green-front lake. Roman gladiators would have understood the pressures; Ryder Cup spectators will relish the contest.

CARD OF THE COURSE

Hole	Distance (yards)	Par
1	465	4
2	610	5
3	189	3
4	461	4
5	457	4
6	452	4
7	213	3
8	439	4
9	666	5
Out	3,952	36
10	210	3
11	562	5
12	458	4
13	189	3
14	413	4
15	377	4
16	508	4
17	211	3
18	613	5
In	3,541	35
Total	**7,493**	**71**

"There's water, drivable par 4s and the finishing stretch is fantastic."

IAN WOOSNAM, CAPTAIN OF EUROPEAN TEAM, 2006 RYDER CUP

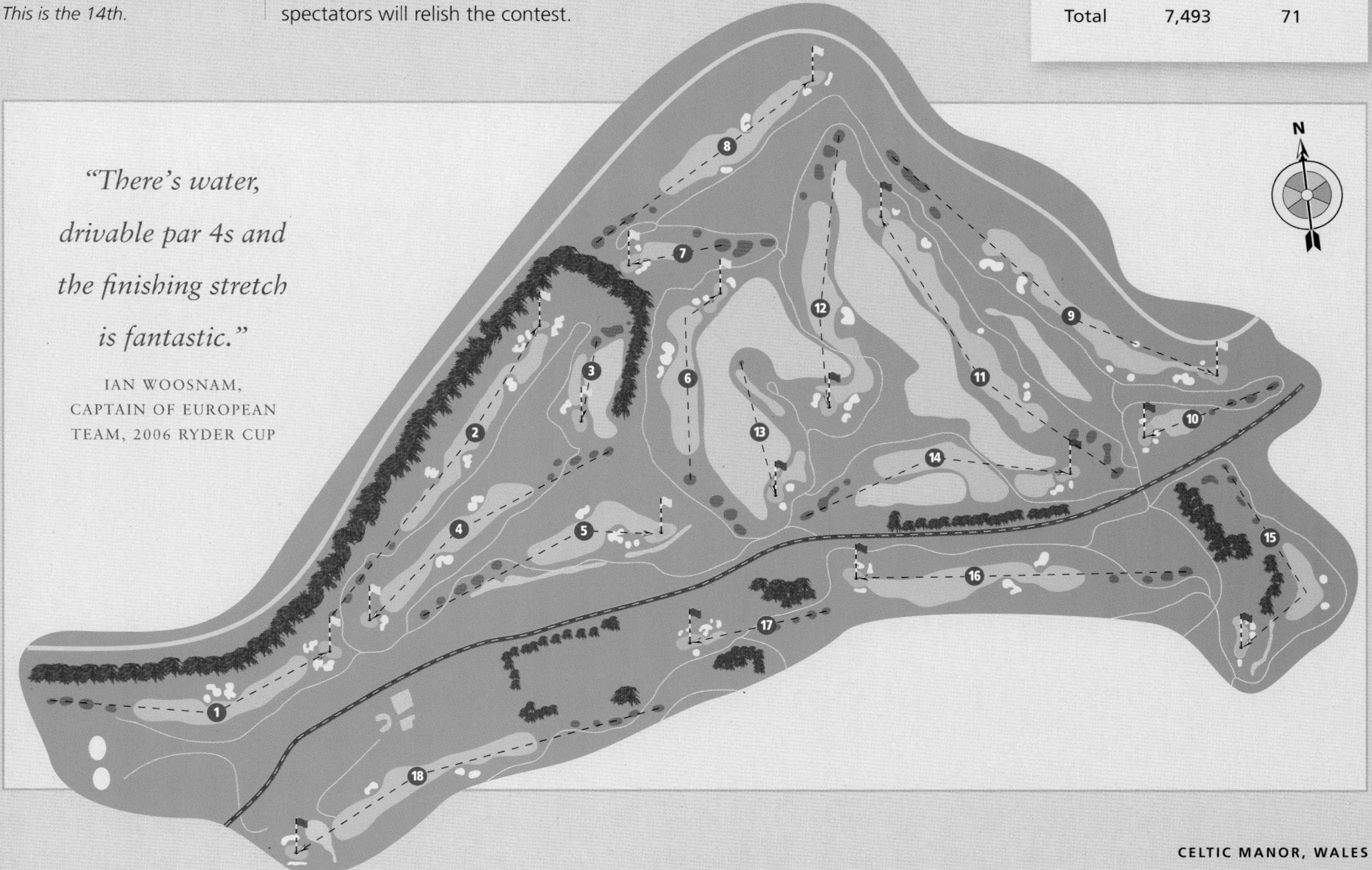

N

Pennard

Pennard

Pennard Golf Club, Southgate, Swansea, West Glamorgan, Wales

Pennard might seem an odd bedfellow for the many longer championship tests in this book, but it claims its place on merit. It is wonderfully scenic, full of character, quirky, and, most of all, enormous fun. What is more, it is a links course yet it is not on a level with the beach but high on the cliffs of the Gower Peninsula overlooking Oxwich Bay.

The club has been in existence since 1896, but it was not until 1908 that James Braid was first called in to lay out an 18-hole course. He returned to make amendments and improvements in 1911, 1920, and 1931. C. K. Cotton and Donald Steel have made significant alterations since then, but the bulk of the course remains Braid's work. Braid's genius was in locating so many very playable holes on such a humpy-bumpy site, nor was he afraid of the unorthodox, which is why the individual holes remain firmly in the mind long after the round is over.

There is never a dull moment on the course, simply because the ground on which it was built has so much movement to it. Even the 1st hole, striking inland away from the sea, is uplifting, with its crinkled fairway down which a long drive is required to get a view of the pin. And the 2nd, the shortest of short holes, is no pushover.

Between church and state

One of Pennard's finest stretches begins on the 6th, which overlooks the ruins of 12th-century Pennard Castle. The 7th, many people's favorite hole, threads a course between the castle and the ruins of a 13th-century church. Heady stuff! Both have brilliantly sited greens. They are followed by another pair of good two-shotters, the 9th being somewhat demanding with its left-turning route countered by its right-leaning fairway.

A par-5, the 10th involves a welcoming downhill drive but a stream crosses the fairway where long hitters would prefer it did not, and there is an uphill approach to the green, made harder by the presence of very visible bunkers. The short 11th is not a Braid hole, but one found by C. K. Cotton in 1965. It is played across a valley to a narrow shelf-green and there are no marks for coming up short. Another

excellent short hole comes at the 13th, again played across a valley to a hilltop green, and there is a lovely view of the castle on its sandy hill to be had from it.

Braid's favorite hole was the 14th, with its drive along a very bouncy fairway and an approach played so steeply uphill that it is like pitching into the sky. Incidentally, in Braid's era there was far less rough than there is today, being instead treacherous exposed sand. Cattle and sheep keep the rough grass in check nowadays. The most spectacular hole is yet to come. It is the 16th, with its magical green position right on the edge of the cliffs overlooking the sea. Incomparable!

One-time Pennard professional Gus Faulkner, father of future British Open champion Max Faulkner, was given permission to shoot rabbits on the course—before 10 a.m.

In the January 1928 edition of *Golf Illustrated*, Sir Ernest Holderness cited the 13th (Castle) as one of the finest holes in Britain.

The distinguished golfer, Vicki Thomas, was a member of Pennard. She played in no fewer than six British Curtis Cup teams.

LEFT *For many, their favorite hole at Pennard is the 7th. What makes Pennard such fun is that the ground has so much character, with never a dull moment.*

CARD OF THE COURSE

Hole	Distance (yards)	Par	Hole	Distance (yards)	Par
1	449	4	10	492	5
2	145	3	11	180	3
3	365	4	12	298	4
4	517	5	13	196	3
5	165	3	14	368	4
6	400	4	15	165	3
7	351	4	16	493	5
8	357	4	17	488	5
9	437	4	18	399	4
Out	3,186	35	In	3,079	36
			Total	**6,265**	**71**

"Pennard is one of my all-time favorites—the site is one of the most spectacular I've ever seen."

TOM DOAK

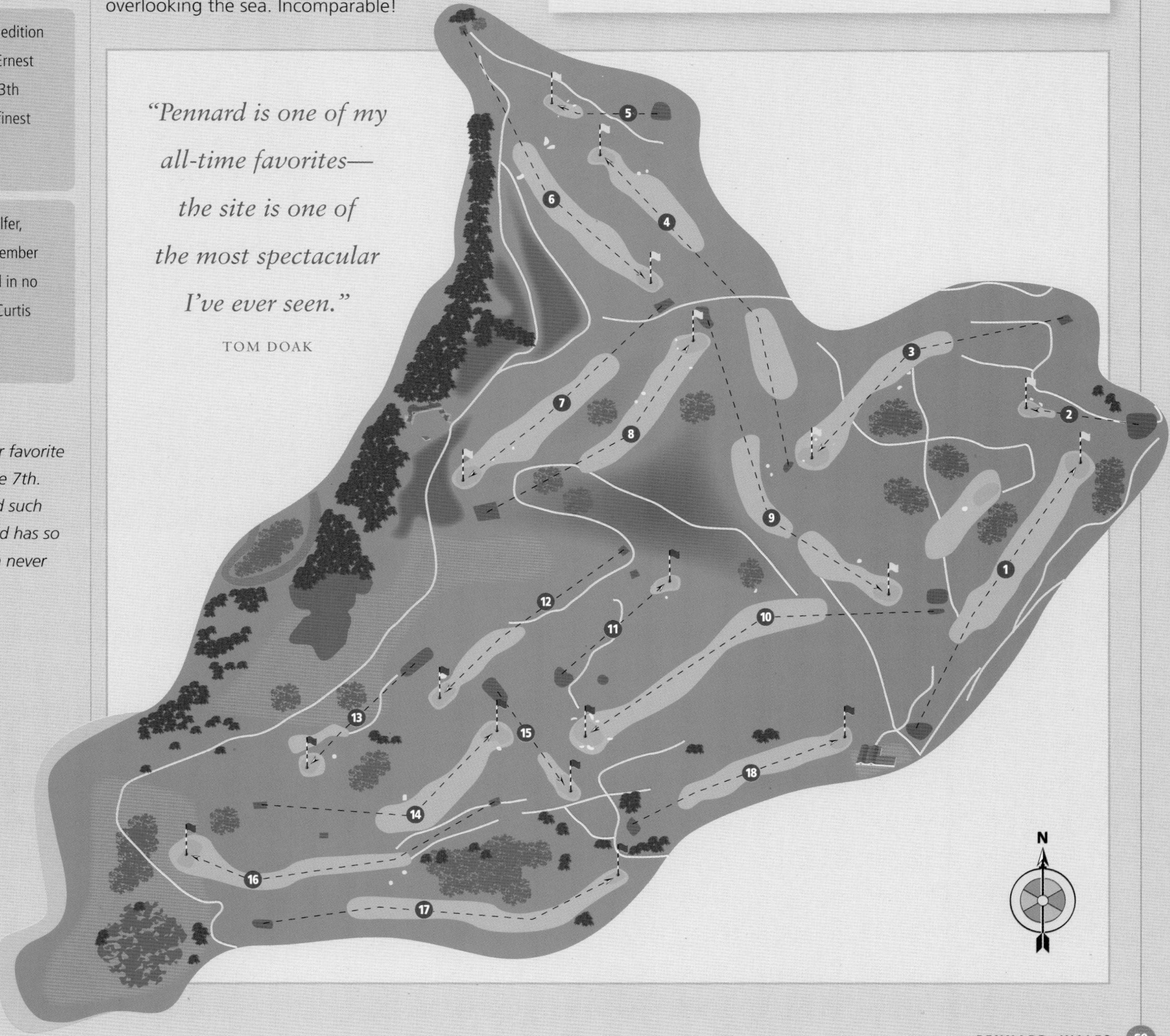

Royal County Down

Royal County Down Golf Club, Newcastle, County Down, Northern Ireland

On the coast of Dundrum Bay, backed by the Mourne Mountains, 18 holes weave purposefully through dunes and gorse to create, in the words of Tom Watson, "a pure links." For over 100 years, Old Tom Morris's routing has changed little, and as such there is a sense that the course has always been here, quietly tucked away in this beautifully unassuming place.

Don't be mistaken in assuming that the age and tradition of the course have left it obsolete in today's game. Though quite capable of hosting major tournaments, Royal County Down has opted to avoid these events, fearing that the course and indigenous wildlife would suffer from trampling spectators and media villages—the Senior British Open and Walker Cup are the biggest events of recent times. It is especially impressive, therefore, that many great players have made the pilgrimage to this wonderful course simply to experience it. Famously, Tiger Woods has chosen these holes to sharpen his links skills before a British Open.

A perfect nine?

The front nine is commonly regarded as the best front nine in golf (not to say that the back nine is shabby). A great starting hole, the par-5 1st is reachable in two, but one must carry the ball long down the left-hand side to take advantage of the sloping fairway, which bounds the ball forward toward the green. As poor drives are punished, with dunes on both sides and the beach on the right, this hole sets the precedent that control is a necessity. Another somewhat daunting feature during the round is that of playing tee shots over dunes, blind or semi-blind.

LEFT *Slieve Donard, the highest of the Mourne Mountains, overlooks Dundrum Bay and the historic Royal County Down links. This is the excellent 3rd hole, viewed from behind the green.*

▶ In 1933, in the Irish Open Amateur Championship, Eric Fiddian recorded two holes-in-one in the final, yet still lost.

After the first couple of drives, which play in the same direction over intimidating hills, when guests reach the 4th tee members often allow them to set up with driver aiming over the dune before pointing out that this is a par 3 played in the opposite direction! Looking in the correct direction from this elevated tee, one is blessed by a gorgeous view of the mountains and sea, but the player can also see the countless challenges ahead. After a carry over gorse bushes, nine brutish bunkers surround a green with large drop-offs to both sides and the back.

Possibly the best hole on the back nine is the 13th. Bunkers plague the dogleg on the right-hand side, and a decent hit down the left is rewarded with lengthy run on the mounds of the firm fairway. If the drive is too short, sight of the green is blocked by the gorse-banked dune on the dogleg. The broad, sloping green is nestled among dunes to create its own amphitheater, backed by swathes of lilac heather. The strength of holes like this, coupled with picturesque scenery and legendary hospitality, have led Royal County Down to a consistent ranking as one of the world's Top 10 courses.

CARD OF THE COURSE

Hole	Distance (yards)	Par
1	539	5
2	444	4
3	477	4
4	213	3
5	440	4
6	398	4
7	145	3
8	430	4
9	486	4
Out	3,572	35
10	197	3
11	440	4
12	527	5
13	444	4
14	212	3
15	467	4
16	337	4
17	435	4
18	550	5
In	3,609	36
Total	7,181	71

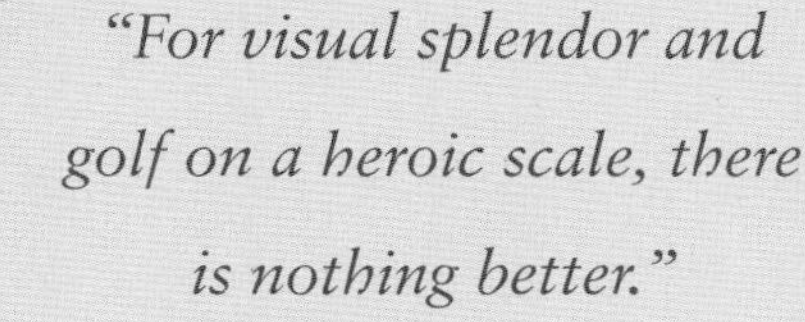

"For visual splendor and golf on a heroic scale, there is nothing better."

DONALD STEEL, *CLASSIC GOLF LINKS OF GREAT BRITAIN AND IRELAND*

BELOW *The bunkers at Royal County Down are serious, both in expanse and depth. Many are topped off by eyebrows of heather or clinging rough grass. These threaten the drive at the 8th.*

Royal Portrush

Dunluce Links, Royal Portrush Golf Club, County Antrim, Northern Ireland

The Dunluce course at Portrush is the only course outside Great Britain to have staged the British Open, which it did once, in 1951, with the dapper Max Faulkner emerging victorious. There is little doubt that the course could still examine the world's best, but the infrastructure of this beautiful corner of Northern Ireland simply could not cope with the huge numbers of visitors, golfers, spectators, and the media that a modern British Open brings.

Royal Portrush is an old club, founded as the County Club in 1888, but its two fine courses (the other being the Valley course) owe their distinction to Harry Colt, who rebuilt and re-routed Old Tom Morris's original course in 1932. What Colt did was golf architecture at its simplest. He noted the parallel lines of sand dunes and routed the holes along the defining valleys between them. His genius, however, was to choose the optimum locations for tees and greens. Indeed, these greens are some of the most testing to find in top-class links golf, despite their having a mere handful of bunkers guarding them. As a result of Colt's cunning use of the shapes of the dunes, none of the par 4s and 5s from the 2nd to the 16th is straight. They all bend one way or another. Dunluce Links is, then, one of the most demanding driving courses in British golf.

A mounting sense of expectation

Even before you reach the course anticipation is eager, the twisting road running along the magnificent rocky coast of County Antrim, past the Giant's Causeway and the ruins of

RIGHT *Colt took full advantage of the nature of the ground at Portrush to create brilliantly sited (and defended) greens, such as the 13th. The Dunluce needs, therefore, fewer bunkers than most other comparable courses.*

▶ The Senior British Open Championship was held at Royal Portrush in 1995. It was won by Brian Barnes, the son-in-law of Max Faulkner, winner of the British Open on the same course in 1951.

▶ Inspired by a new putter, Max Faulkner led the field after the second round and was flamboyantly signing autographs "Open Champion 1951." Despite tempting fate so extravagantly, he did indeed go on to win.

Dunluce Castle. Suddenly, round a bend, you espy the courses for the first time, and the sight is thrilling. Even the most experienced links golfer cannot fail to be excited by the tumbling nature of the ground and the broad seascape.

The course, too, builds over the first few holes, until on the 5th tee you stand overlooking a distant fairway angled away to the right towards a green located on the very edge of the Atlantic Ocean. Visually, it is a stunning hole, but already the screw is being turned. That hole had no need of bunkers, nor do two of the best short holes, the 6th and 14th. A full carry over inhospitable low ground is required to reach the plateau green of the 6th, the hole that carries the name of its architect, Harry Colt.

Calamity is the name of the 14th, probably the most famous hole at Portrush. It is an appropriate name if you come up short or, worse, down in the abyss on the right—woe betide those plagued by a slice. This hole is perhaps as near as you can get to a dogleg par 3! You have to aim left and allow the ground in front of the green to feed the ball to the right. A good, traditional ground-game shot is what is required here, and at a little over 200 yards/183 m a sound technique is demanded. Foozling does not work at Portrush!

CARD OF THE COURSE

Hole	*Distance (yards)*	*Par*	*Hole*	*Distance (yards)*	*Par*
1	392	4	10	478	5
2	505	5	11	170	3
3	155	3	12	392	4
4	457	4	13	386	4
5	384	4	14	210	3
6	189	3	15	365	4
7	431	4	16	428	4
8	384	4	17	548	5
9	475	5	18	469	4
Out	3,372	36	In	3,446	36
			Total	**6,818**	**72**

"Portrush is flying golf—one longs to take off after the ball."

PATRIC DICKINSON, *A ROUND OF GOLF COURSES*

Ballybunion

The Old Course, Ballybunion, County Kerry, Republic of Ireland

A round of golf on the Old Course at Ballybunion is a unique experience. None other than Tom Watson would agree. He was very much responsible for alerting the world to the existence of this extraordinary place, which was largely unknown outside Ireland when he first visited in 1981. Now acknowledged as one of the world's greatest courses, many a star golfer has made the pilgrimage to play it.

Ballybunion is a long-established club, founded in 1893 in the far west of Ireland on a stretch of quite incomparable dunes overlooking the Atlantic Ocean. There are many golf courses in the west of Ireland set on dunes overlooking the Atlantic, but what sets Ballybunion apart is the way the course is routed over, through, across, and along the dunes. So the golfer is asked to play a huge catalog of different shots throughout the round to adapt to the constantly changing topography.

COASTAL EROSION

It is the stuff of nightmares—seeing your course washed away by the unstoppable power of the sea. The venerable Olympic Club in San Francisco lost a number of holes to the Pacific Ocean some years ago. Ballybunion, too, faced the prospect of losing some of its finest holes to the Atlantic Ocean in the 1970s. An appeal was launched, and that was when Ballybunion found that it had friends, generous ones, all over the world. With the threat of global warming raising sea levels, erosion is on many clubs' agendas throughout the world.

BELOW *The full might, majesty, dominion, and power of Ballybunion, as portrayed by the conjunction of the wonderfully sited 10th green and beyond it the magical 11th fairway.*

▶ Ballybunion was enlarged into an 18-hole course in 1926. The "designer" was a Mr. Smyth. His layout was so good that when Tom Simpson was engaged to upgrade it in 1937 he suggested only three minor changes.

▶ Ballybunion is so far from any major population center that it has hosted the Irish Open only once, in 2000. Sweden's Patrik Sjöland emerged victorious after opening rounds of 64 and 65.

Natural hazards

The Old Course excites golfers of all abilities. The round starts ominously, for there is a graveyard awaiting the merest slice from the 1st tee, and from here to the corner of the dogleg on the 6th the course slides into gear rather as an Irish morning slowly gathers momentum. At this point the adrenaline kicks in, with a delicious pitch up to a green on top of the dunes, the first of a series of greens that seriously tests every department of the approach game. This hole has no need of a bunker and, once away from the opening (inland) holes, there are remarkably few bunkers on the course as a whole. Such is the brilliance of the green sites that grassy swales and fall-aways protect the holes even more strongly than sand would.

Indeed, one of the finest holes on the course—one of the world's great holes—has no bunker, either. It is the unforgettable 11th, a gorgeous hole tumbling down through the sand hills alongside the Atlantic with a green cleverly defended by encircling dunes. There are great holes still to come, but it was the short 8th that particularly appealed to Watson on his first visit, with an all-or-nothing shot to a tiny green and desperate recovery work required should the tee shot fail to hold the putting surface.

Ballybunion boasts back-to-back par 3s on the inward half, the 14th and 15th. Like every hole here, they were dictated naturally by the exciting land forms, and the 15th is a great short hole, played to a marvelous green backed by the Atlantic Ocean. Then the excellent 16th and 17th both make excursions to the oceanside. Ballybunion should be on every golfer's must-play list.

CARD OF THE COURSE

Hole	Distance (yards)	Par
1	392	4
2	445	4
3	220	3
4	498	5
5	508	5
6	364	4
7	423	4
8	153	3
9	454	4
Out	3,457	36
10	359	4
11	449	4
12	192	3
13	484	5
14	131	3
15	216	3
16	490	5
17	385	4
18	379	4
In	3,085	35
Total	6,542	71

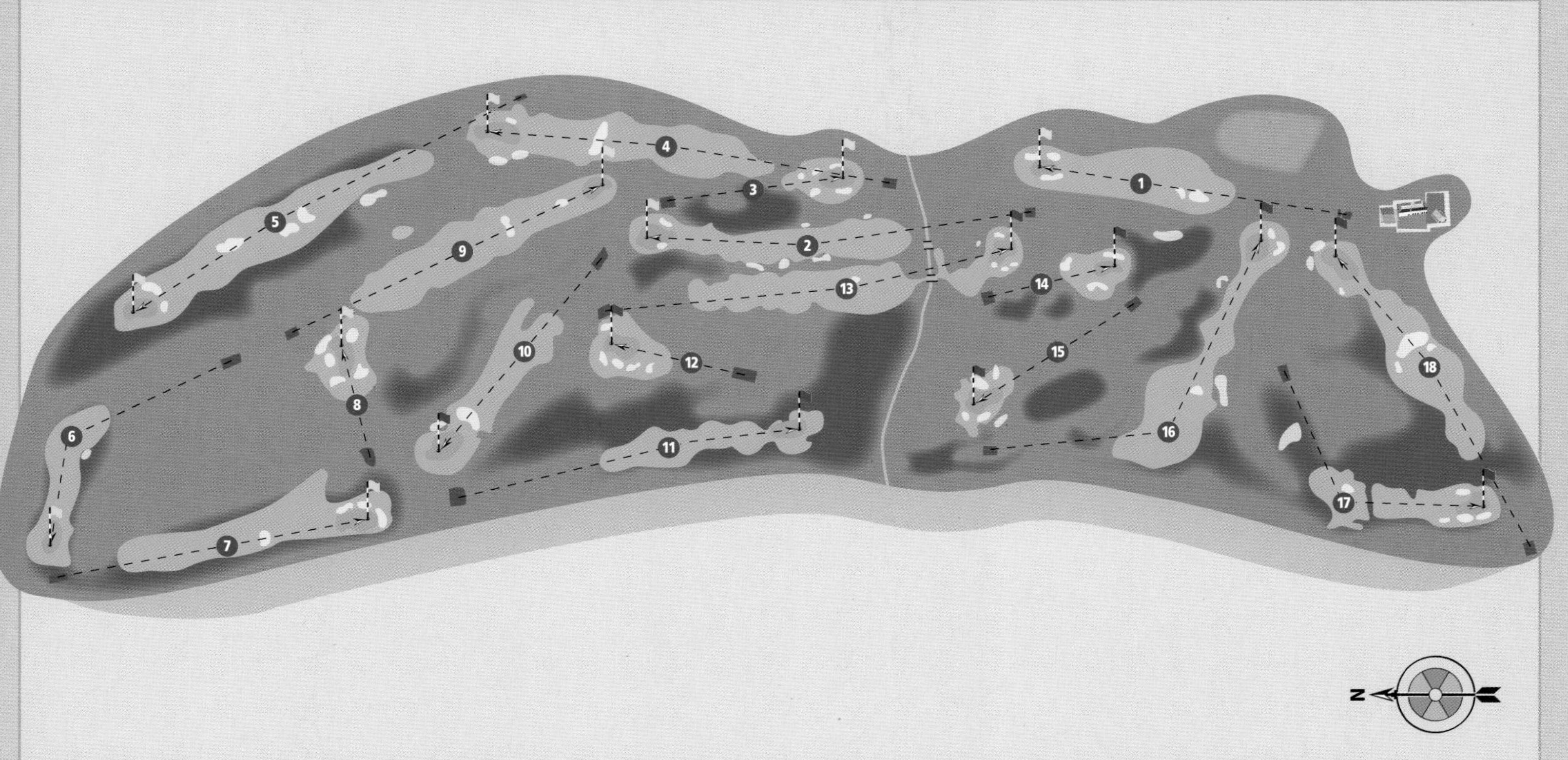

FINEST PIECE OF LINKSLAND

In the late 1960s the decision was taken to purchase further duneland to the south of the existing links. By 1980 sufficient funds had been raised to consider building a second course, and Robert Trent Jones was approached. He wrote, "I was given both a once-in-a-lifetime opportunity and a terrifying challenge . . . the property I had to work with is perhaps the finest piece of linksland in the world." In 1984 the Cashen Course was completed, but it is proving to be controversial. Jones made spectacular use of the site, but the course is too hard for higher-handicap players. That said, the Cashen possesses a fabulous collection of green sites, and Ballybunion as a whole offers a wonderful test of approach work.

RIGHT *Tom Watson rated the 11th "one of the toughest holes in the world . . . a small target with not a lot of room to miss right or left."*

Lahinch

Old Course, Lahinch Golf Club, County Clare, Republic of Ireland

Lahinch! Now there's a place to set the romantic golfer's heart racing. Locals think of Lahinch as the Irish St. Andrews, and they have a point. This town simply exists for golf—that is untrue, of course, but it feels as if it does. And Old Tom Morris came all the way here from St. Andrews more than 100 years ago to develop its earliest course into what might be described as its first proper course.

Erosion of parts of the course and the desire by the members for something even better brought Alister MacKenzie to the town in 1927 to give the course a revamp, which turned out to be a very substantially new course, with only a few holes retained—but what classics they have proved to be. It was one of MacKenzie's very few forays into links golf, although he loved the medium, always citing the Old Course at St. Andrews as the model for all principles of golf design.

Alas, MacKenzie's course did not survive intact. Erosion again damaged parts of the course and lesser replacements were constructed. It was still a good course, but it was no longer in the very top flight. In 1999 the club decided to remedy the situation, and this time it was Martin Hawtree who was given the responsibility of putting Lahinch once again alongside Portmarnock and Ballybunion at the pinnacle of links golf in the Republic. He succeeded impressively.

Lahinch is blessed with such fabulous dunes that any course laid out on them would be at least good, and, given the pedigree of the architects who have worked here, it is no surprise that it is exceptionally good. There are many world-class holes, and the 3rd, 6th, 7th, 9th, 10th, 14th, 15th, and 17th can hold their heads up among the strongest par 4s anywhere. Furthermore, that 7th is one of two Hawtree holes, along with the 11th, which have opened up stunning seascapes lost for many years. And, for good measure, the 13th is one of the most delightful short par 4s imaginable—drivable perhaps, but with any number of ways of making you feel foolish if you do not succeed.

Klondyke and the Dell

Yet it is for two particularly anachronistic holes, the 4th and 5th, that Lahinch is perhaps best known. The former is known as Klondyke after the giant sand hill of that name that interrupts the fairway most of the way to the green. Those hoping for an eagle must play their second shot blind over it. It is not any easier to try to go round it. To make matters even worse, the green is hard up against a grassy bank beyond which is out of bounds. That eagle-seeking second shot must be hit absolutely spot-on.

If that were not enough, the 5th, Dell, is a short hole played entirely blind across a high sand dune to a sunken green on the far side. It has been left unaltered from Tom Morris's course, a charming reminder of days gone by. And if that were not enough, the tee shot on the final hole is played by crossing over both the 4th and 5th holes!

▶ Lahinch's weather forecasting is tried and tested: members observe the local goats that roam freely on the dunes. If they are out on the course, the weather will be fine. If they are up by the clubhouse, you may expect a downpour.

LEFT *Lahinch enjoys linksland of real character—humps and bumps all over the place. The crisp seaside turf makes the playing of all manner of shots a genuine pleasure.*

CARD OF THE COURSE

Hole	Distance (yards)	Par
1	381	4
2	534	5
3	446	4
4	475	5
5	154	3
6	424	4
7	411	4
8	166	3
9	400	4
Out	3,391	36
10	441	4
11	170	3
12	577	5
13	279	4
14	461	4
15	466	4
16	195	3
17	436	4
18	534	5
In	3,559	37
Total	**6,950**	**72**

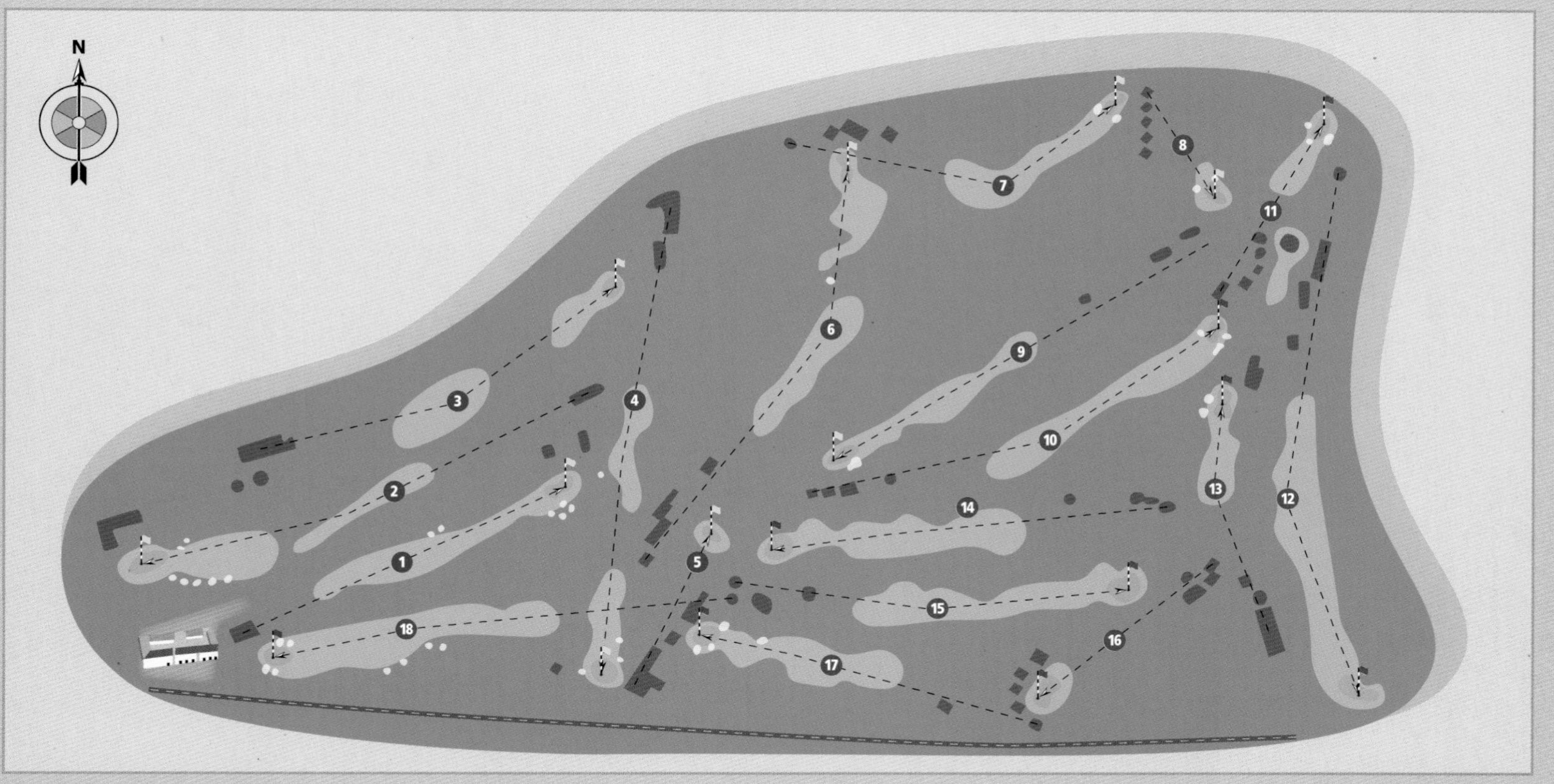

Old Head

Old Head Golf Links, Kinsale, County Cork, Republic of Ireland

If you suffer from vertigo or are strapped for cash think twice about visiting Old Head. It stands high above the Atlantic Ocean, with sheer cliffs plunging straight down into the pounding waves, and it boasts one of the highest green fees in Europe. Nevertheless, Old Head is a course no golfer should pass up an opportunity to play.

Old Head is a historic place, recorded in a map of AD 100 by the Egyptian mathematician Ptolemy. The Eirinn clan settled there in 900 BC, giving their name to Ireland. In 1915 the British liner *Lusitania* was torpedoed just off the headland by a German submarine, with the loss of over 1,000 lives. That incident was partly responsible for the United States entering World War I.

The atmosphere is set right from the outset when you approach the club through the ruins of a 12th-century tower. You will come across the remains of 17th- and 19th-century lighthouses as you play the 7th. But that will do for history, for what bowls the visitor over is the breathtaking setting. And because there is only just room enough for 18 holes on the headland every inch of ground is used, giving no fewer than nine holes clinging to the edge of the cliffs.

Brothers John and Patrick O'Connor bought this land in 1989, and it took four years to overcome objections before construction could commence, with the course finally opening in 1997. A raft of wise heads was engaged to design the course: Ron Kirby (who had been part of the Nicklaus design team), Paddy Merrigan (a Cork-based architect), Eddie Hackett (the talented and prolific Irish architect), Joe Carr (Ireland's greatest amateur player), and Liam Higgins (professional at Waterville).

Their biggest requirement was restraint—not of budget, but of exuberance, for the wind blows hard here almost every day, so greens could not be heavily contoured and fairways needed to be generously wide. Even so, it is a rare day when a four-ball manages to get round the course without losing boxfuls of golf balls to the Atlantic.

RIGHT *The wicked 4th fairway, clinging to the clifftop as it makes its ever-narrowing way to the distant green, itself perched right on the edge above the Atlantic.*

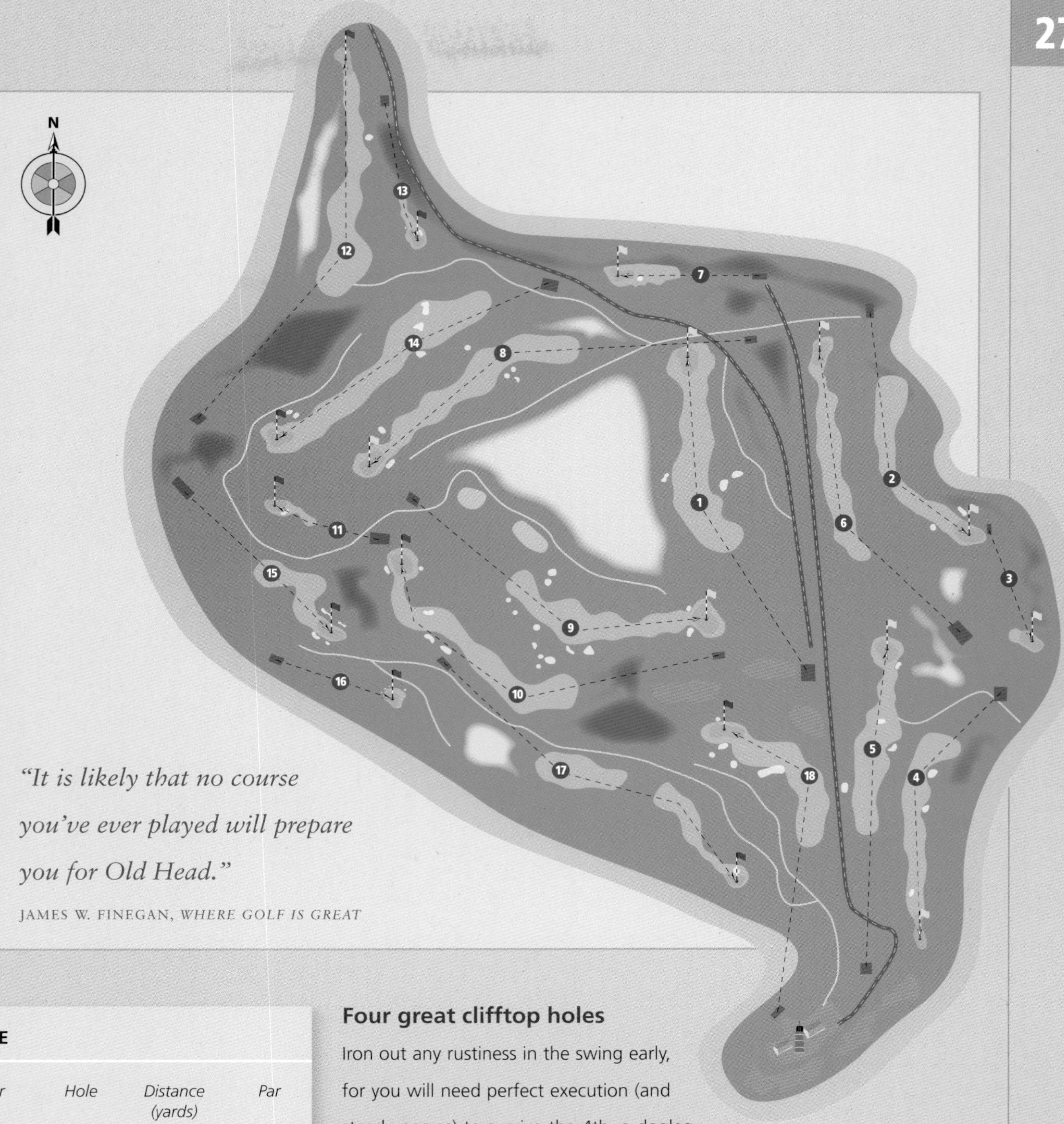

▶ Old Head was designed to be played at widely differing lengths, according to the golfer's ability. Consequently there are at least six separate teeing grounds on every hole.

▶ Kinsale has a reputation as the food capital of Ireland and hosts an international food festival each October.

"It is likely that no course you've ever played will prepare you for Old Head."

JAMES W. FINEGAN, *WHERE GOLF IS GREAT*

CARD OF THE COURSE

Hole	Distance (yards)	Par	Hole	Distance (yards)	Par
1	446	4	10	518	5
2	406	4	11	198	3
3	178	3	12	564	5
4	427	4	13	258	3
5	430	4	14	452	4
6	495	5	15	342	4
7	192	3	16	190	3
8	549	5	17	632	5
9	475	4	18	460	4
Out	3,598	36	In	3,614	36
			Total	7,212	72

Four great clifftop holes

Iron out any rustiness in the swing early, for you will need perfect execution (and steady nerves) to survive the 4th, a dogleg played from a clifftop tee to a narrow fairway threatened by cliffs on the left all the way to a green raised up and perched directly on the cliff's edge, overlooked by the lighthouse of 1853 vintage, a constant reminder of the dangerous nature of these treacherous waters. You will be required to drive across a corner of the cliffs on the par-5 12th, and, once again, the green clings perilously to the edge of the cliffs—no place for a left-handed slicer! That is true also of the 13th, a long par 3 with yet another wonderfully sited green on high ground with the now almost obligatory drop to perdition on the left.

Finally in these world-class holes there is the 17th, another par 5, this time falling to a green set at the end of a long descent with the ocean, on this occasion, a constant threat on the right.

Courses 28–46

U.S.A.

28 Augusta, Georgia
29 Bethpage, New York
30 Kapalua, Hawaii
31 Kiawah Island, South Carolina
32 Merion, Pennsylvania
33 Oakmont, Pennsylvania
34 Pebble Beach, California
35 Pine Valley, New Jersey
36 Pinehurst, North Carolina
37 Shinnecock Hills, New York
38 Torrey Pines, California
39 TPC Sawgrass, Florida
40 TPC Scottsdale, Arizona
41 Valhalla, Kentucky
42 Whistling Straits, Wisconsin
43 Winged Foot, New York

CANADA

44 Banff Springs, Alberta
45 Highland Links, Nova Scotia
46 St. George's, Ontario

North America

Is there a greater golfing nation than the United States? The answer has to be no. It has produced more world-class golfers, and has more golf clubs and courses, than any other country, and the number and variety of its golf resorts is amazing. Through its huge buying power it could change the whole nature of golf, yet it readily embraces the traditional: Merion, Shinnecock Hills, Augusta National—great courses and, importantly, great clubs.

In most respects Canada is similar, except that its golfing season is curtailed by the severity of its winter. However, Canada can claim to have beaten the United States to forming a properly constituted golf club, Montreal Golf Club (later Royal) having been founded in 1873.

A word of caution: unlike in most of the rest of the world, where a visitor can often turn up, pay a green fee, and play almost any course, in North America many clubs are strictly private—the only visitors allowed being members' guests. However, the good news is that public-access courses are plentiful, and resort courses include some of the finest in the world.

Augusta

Augusta National Golf Club, Georgia, U.S.A.

Tennis at Wimbledon or Flushing Meadow, motor racing at Le Mans or Indianapolis, racing at Longchamp or Churchill Downs, golf at St. Andrews or . . . ? Most people, even those who have little knowledge of golf, would probably answer, "Augusta National." Its modern-day fame comes from its hosting of the Masters, the first major of the professional golfing year, and the only major held annually on the same course. But that fame would not have arisen had it not been for one Robert Tyre Jones, or Bobby or Bob, depending on which side of the Atlantic you come from.

Jones was the greatest amateur golfer of all time, winning five U.S. Amateur titles and one Amateur Championship in Britain. But he was also good enough to take on and beat the best professionals of the day (the 1920s) taking the U.S. Open on four occasions and the British Open on three. Having won the Amateur and Open Championships of America and Britain in the same year, 1930, he retired from competitive golf, much to the relief of the rest of them!

BELOW *Catch your drive perfectly and you can take advantage of this downslope to reduce the playing length of the 10th hole significantly. The raised green is not one to miss.*

Jones's unlikely design partner

When Jones came to establish his ideal golf course, on which he and his wealthy friends might play, he had some novel ideas about how it might be set up, making the best players feel seriously tested while somehow allowing the high-handicapper to get round in 100 or so without feeling like abandoning golf for good. And it was a pure accident that led Jones to find the ideal architect to help him realize this concept. In 1929 Jones had been knocked out of the U.S. Amateur Championship unexpectedly early. That year the event was held at Pebble Beach, California, so he took the

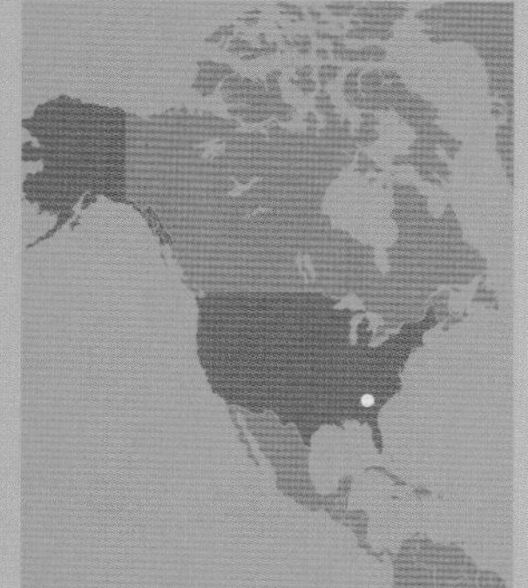

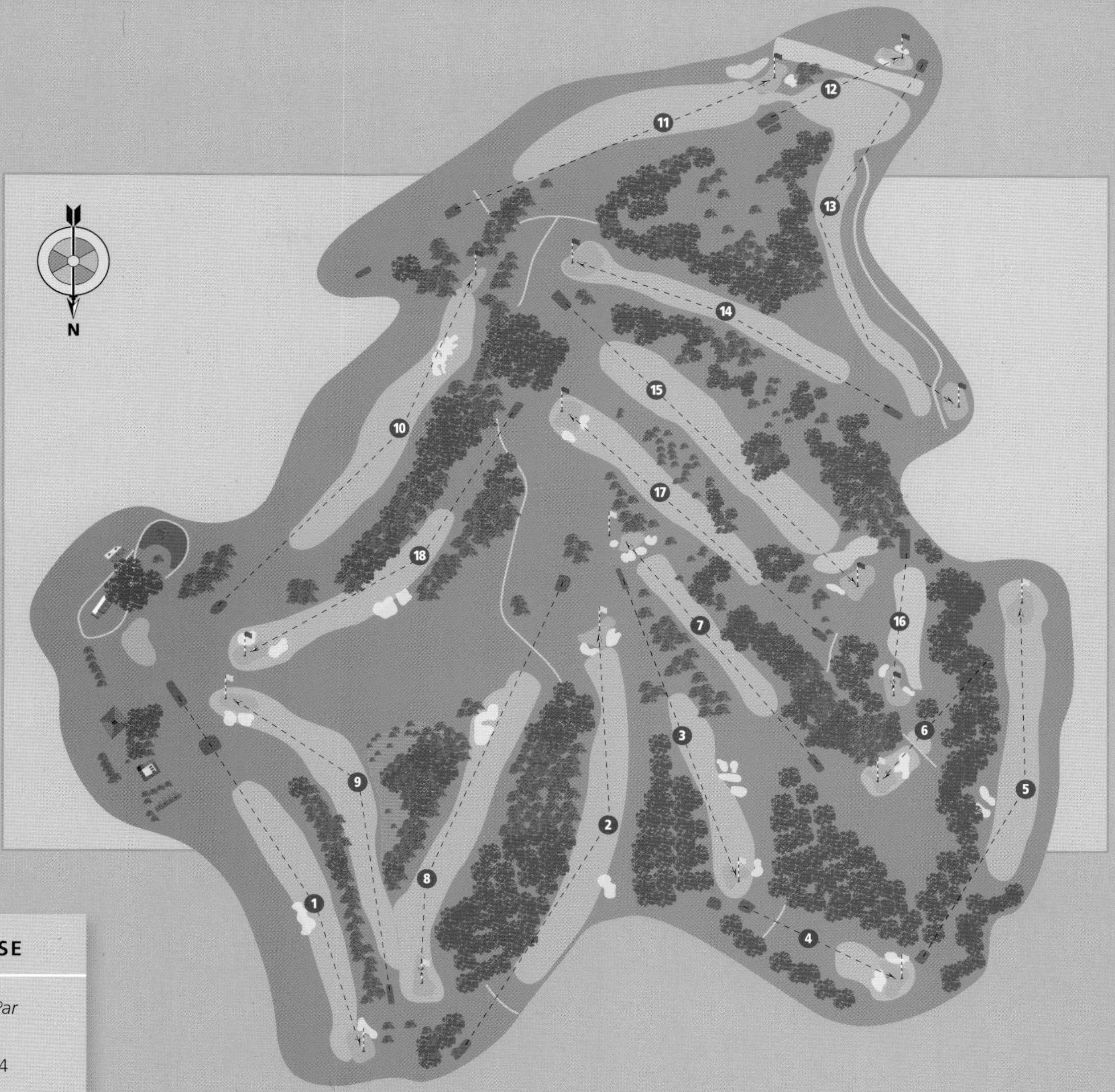

CARD OF THE COURSE

Hole	Distance (yards)	Par
1	435	4
2	575	5
3	350	4
4	205	3
5	455	4
6	180	3
7	410	4
8	570	5
9	460	4
Out	3,640	36
10	495	4
11	490	4
12	155	3
13	510	5
14	440	4
15	500	5
16	170	3
17	425	4
18	465	4
In	3,650	36
Total	7,290	72

opportunity to play nearby Cypress Point and Pasatiempo, both courses designed by Alister MacKenzie, a Leeds physician turned golf course architect—one of the very best in fact. Jones knew immediately that he had found the right man for the job.

Although today's course is little altered from the original (a new 16th hole and revisions to the bunkering) it is set up for the Masters in a manner far removed from what Jones or MacKenzie could have anticipated. Quite simply, the greens are maintained at frighteningly fast speeds, and trees and rough have been planted where previously there were neither. It provides a spectacle for television and it prevents scores becoming ridiculously low, but no high-handicapper would survive a hole, let alone 18!

Yet it remains a fabulous (and fabulously beautiful) course. How often we viewers are on tenterhooks as the leaders pass through the treacherous Amen Corner (11th, 12th, and 13th holes) with Rae's Creek awaiting just the tiniest slipup. Will they risk all and try to get on the 13th and 15th greens in two? And there are—to us—impossible putts on the 16th and 17th greens. Or how about that slick, downhill 8-footer on the last green that must go in or we are into a play-off? The Masters is always dramatic.

▸ Augusta is ablaze with azaleas during the Masters. Before it was a golf course, this was a nursery, Fruitlands, owned by a Belgian horticulturalist, Baron Berckmans, who popularized the azalea in America.

▸ When Tiger Woods won the 2001 Masters he became the first player to hold all four majors at the same time (having won the U.S. Open, British Open and USPGA the previous year). He was 65 under par for the four tournaments.

A COVETED INVITATION

The Masters is unique among the majors for having an invited field of under 100 competitors of whom a number will be amateurs. The spectators, too, are a select group, tickets being guarded jealously by those lucky enough to have them, for they are not available for public sale, and any spectator behaving in an inappropriate or unsporting manner will have their ticket confiscated in what is effectively a life ban. Consequently the same patrons return year after year, their collective experience adding to their generous support for every player, giving the Masters' galleries a deserved reputation for knowledgeable and considerate support. In this, of course, they are upholding the traditions for sportsmanship embodied by Bob Jones.

The 13th (below), 16th (main picture), and 12th (top right) are favorite holes with Masters' spectators, for each hole witnesses great drama every day: an unlikely birdie or eagle, perhaps, or an undesired skirmish with the water and a rapid tumble down the leader board.

Bethpage

Bethpage

Black Course, Bethpage State Park, New York, U.S.A.

Bethpage Black was the first truly public golf facility to host the U.S. Open. True, Pebble Beach and Pinehurst are open to the public, but they are very expensive resort courses. As competitors in the 2002 U.S. Open can testify, it is a fearsome course—long, demanding, and punishing. Hardly surprisingly, the man who had the best answers to the questions posed was Tiger Woods. So successful was the 2002 U.S. Open that it has already been scheduled to host the 2009 event—a remarkably swift return.

Golf owes a huge debt of gratitude to one Robert Moses. He was the Commissioner of New York's State Parks in the dark years of the Great Depression. What was so remarkable about him was that he had the vision, as well as the political know-how (or sheer willpower, perhaps), to get three brand new golf courses of the highest class constructed in Bethpage State Park in the 1930s. Additionally he had an existing one on the site upgraded, and, for the record, a fifth course was added in the 1950s, all for the benefit of metropolitan golfers who could not afford (or did not have the required connections) to be members of a private club. So marvelous were these courses that they were soon being enjoyed for a modest green fee by many members of wealthy (but architecturally inferior) clubs.

Moses had the wisdom to employ the formidable Albert Warren Tillinghast as his architect of choice. Tillinghast did not moderate his design thoughts just because this was a public facility.

Sandy wastes

Tillinghast was given free run of a vast tract of sandy woodland with enough change of level to afford him plenty of natural sites for the greens. He plotted a route through the trees, felled no more than he had to, and liberally sprinkled the whole thing with formidable bunkers of huge proportions. So the course is narrow, calling for arrow-like shots to pierce the gaps in the trees and howitzer-like trajectories to find the few benign bits of fairway not otherwise occupied by sandy wastelands.

A glance at the card is sufficient to reveal that the strength of the course comes in its long two-shot holes, particularly over the back nine, with perhaps the 15th the most difficult hole on the course. Tillinghast's short holes are invariably demanding, and those at Bethpage Black

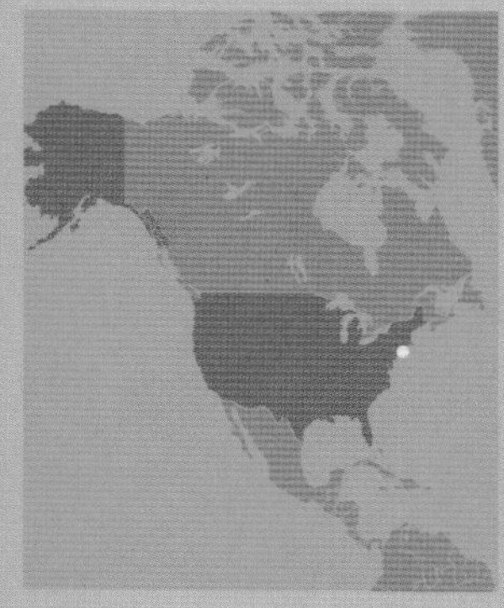

do not disappoint, with the heavily bunkered 17th giving no respite on what is an exhausting home run. Oddly enough the weakest hole may be the last, even after Rees Jones lengthened it for the 2002 U.S. Open.

Interestingly, one of the best holes at Bethpage is the 4th, a par 5 of only 517 yards/ 473 m, surely easily reached in two shots by today's powerful players. But that is to ignore the difficulty of the drive, which is influenced by a bunker on the left of the fairway. Quite simply, if the green is to be reached in two, the drive must clear this on the most precise line imaginable. To balance that drive, Tillinghast calls for something similar on the next hole, but this time placing the compulsory bunker carry on the right of the fairway. He never lets up—which is why Tiger Woods with his superior powers of concentration was always likely to come out on top.

CARD OF THE COURSE

Hole	*Distance (yards)*	*Par*	*Hole*	*Distance (yards)*	*Par*
1	430	4	10	492	4
2	389	4	11	435	4
3	205	3	12	499	4
4	517	5	13	554	4
5	451	4	14	161	3
6	408	4	15	478	4
7	553	5	16	479	4
8	210	3	17	207	3
9	418	4	18	411	4
Out	3,581	36	In	3,716	35
			Total	**7,297**	**71**

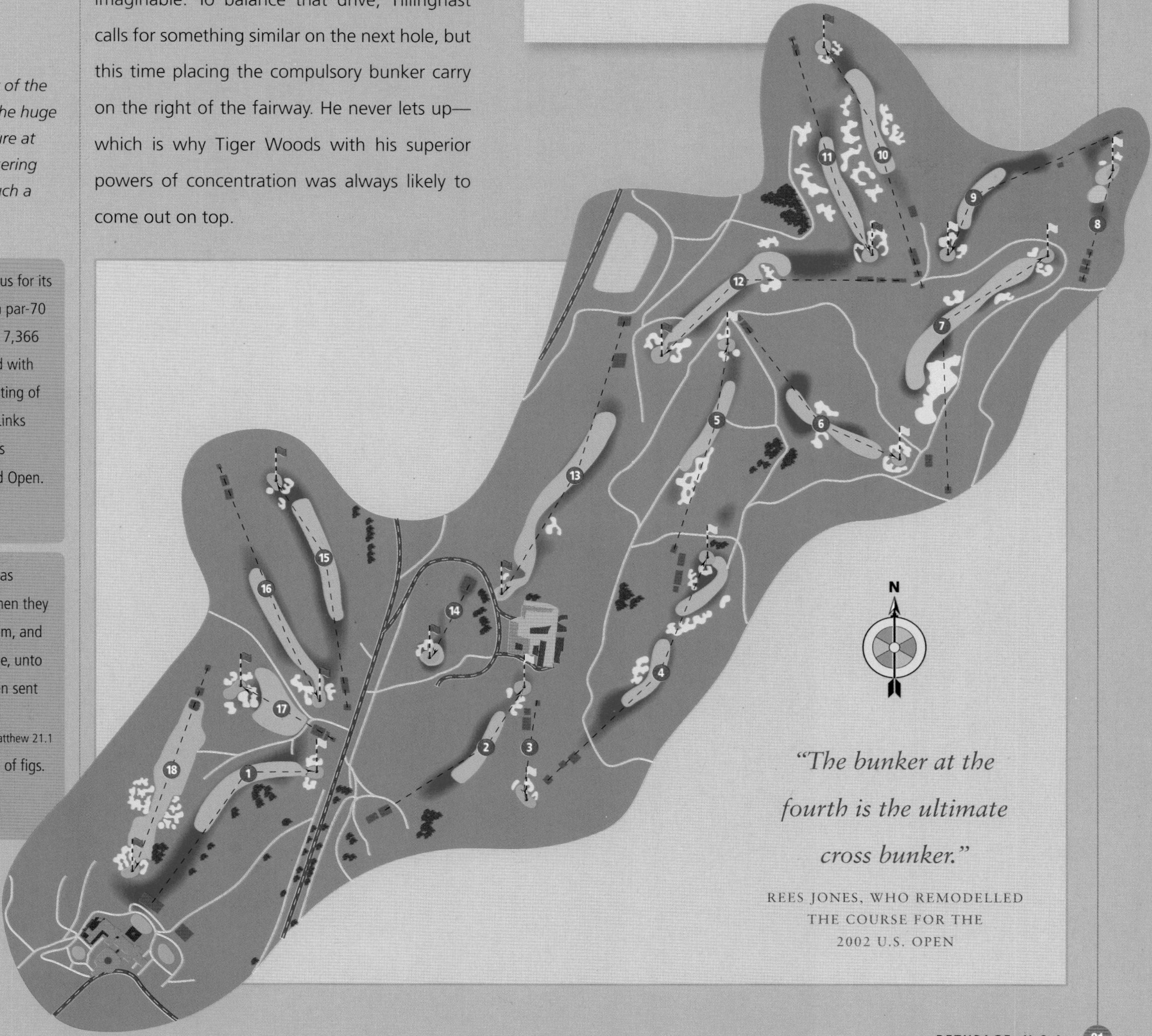

LEFT *This aerial view of the 4th hole shows well the huge scale of the architecture at Bethpage Black. Bunkering of this kind is very much a Tillinghast trademark.*

▶ The Red Course, famous for its tough opening hole, is a par-70 championship course of 7,366 yards/6,735 m. It shared with the Blue Course the hosting of the 1936 USGA Public Links Championship and hosts annually the Long Island Open.

▶ The name Bethpage has Biblical origins: "And when they drew nigh unto Jerusalem, and were come to Bethphage, unto the mount of Olives, then sent Jesus two disciples . . ."
St. Matthew 21.1
Bethphàge means place of figs.

"The bunker at the fourth is the ultimate cross bunker."

REES JONES, WHO REMODELLED THE COURSE FOR THE 2002 U.S. OPEN

Kapalua

Kapalua

Plantation Course, Kapalua Resort, Maui, Hawaii, U.S.A.

You could be forgiven for thinking that the Plantation Course at Kapalua is something of a monster, boasting as it does the longest hole on the U.S. PGA Tour. The 18th hole measures a mind-boggling 663 yards/606 m, yet it is regularly reached in two shots by today's mighty hitters. It does not bear thinking about! In fact the course is anything but a monster. The Plantation Course is a thing of rare beauty.

Kapalua Resort already boasted two Arnold Palmer-designed tracks, the Village and Bay courses, when the fledgling design team of Ben Crenshaw and Bill Coore were approached to build a third course over an upland site offering magnificent vistas and enough character in the landform to excite these two perfectionist craftsmen. They do not bludgeon courses out of the earth with mighty earthmovers and vast quantities of dynamite. They handcraft them. Their later work at Sand Hills (Nebraska), Friars Head (New York), Cuscowilla (Georgia), and Bandon Trails (Oregon) has been recognized by knowledgeable golfers and the golfing press as being world-class. The Plantation Course, only their second full 18-hole design, opened in 1991, has proved its merit each year since 1999 as the venue for the Mercedes-Benz Championship, which opens the Tour year in January, bringing together the winners of each of the previous season's tournaments.

Wind factor

Glance at the card of the course and you'll be forgiven for thinking that it is littered with misprints. Take the 1st, for instance, an apparently unreachable par 4 of 520 yards/475 m. Yet the architects routed the course so that this hole takes full advantage of a following wind, so the hole turns out to be perfectly reachable. In contrast, the 13th is a par 4 of a mere 407 yards/372 m, yet it turns out to be the most difficult hole on the course. Why? Because it plays directly

RIGHT *The 18th hole on the Plantation Course at Kapalua, the longest hole on the U.S. Tour, yet entirely in keeping with the glorious scenery that forms its backdrop.*

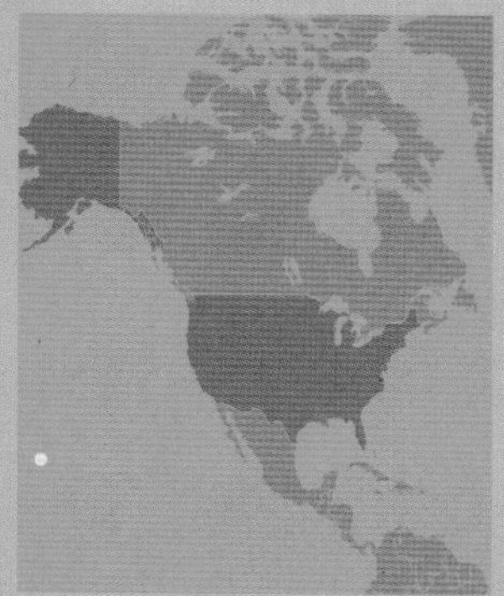

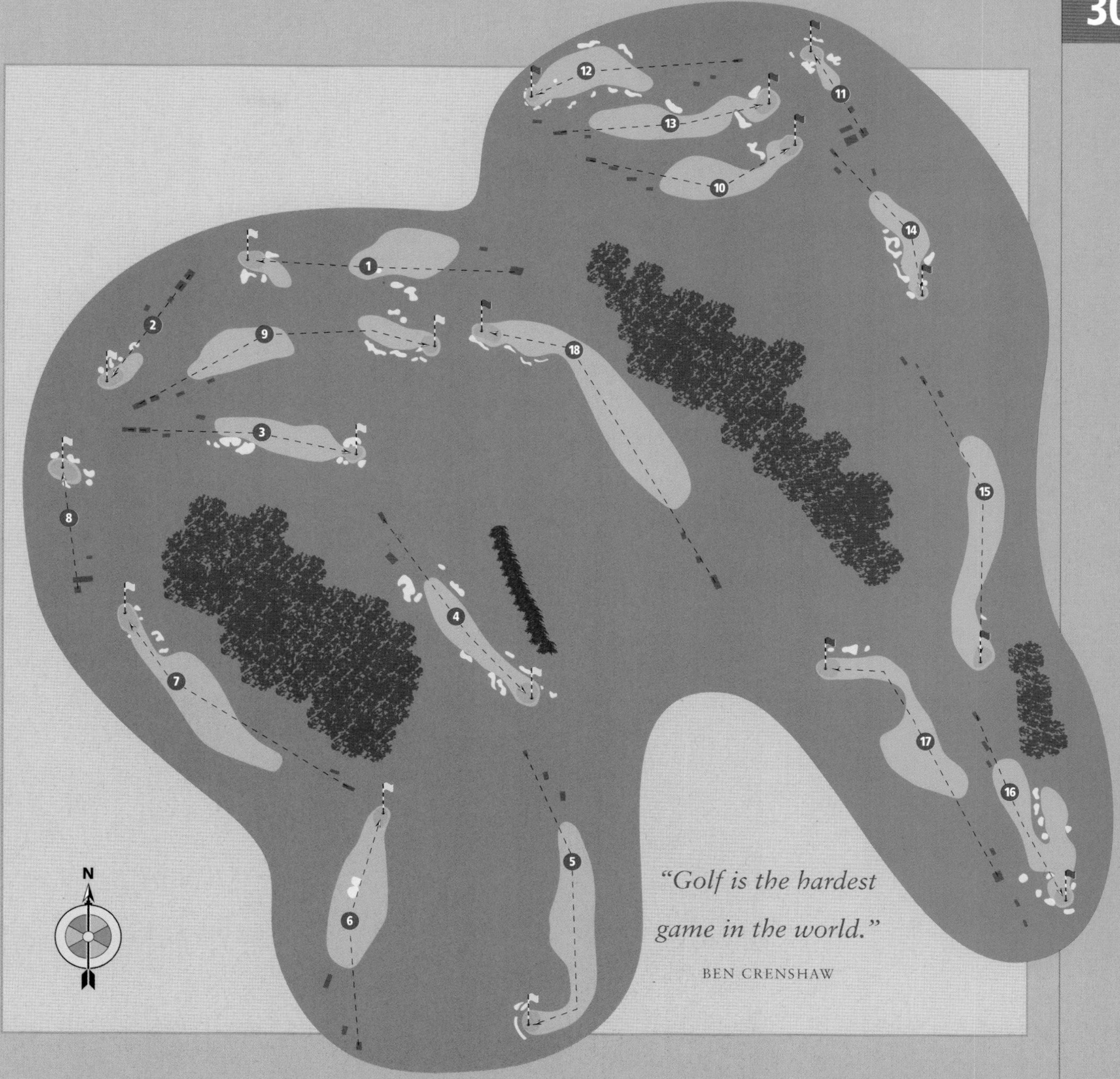

▶ Arnold Palmer's Bay Course offers an alternative to those not quite up to the challenge of the Plantation Course's considerable length. Although measuring 6,600 yards/6,035 m from the back tees there are only two par 4s in excess of 400 yards/366 m.

▶ The Plantation Course is unusual in having only three short holes, but they are among the most difficult on the course. Aiming straight at the pin will bring disaster. With wind a constant factor, they require you to drift or shape the ball into the green.

"Golf is the hardest game in the world."

BEN CRENSHAW

CARD OF THE COURSE

Hole	Distance (yards)	Par	Hole	Distance (yards)	Par
1	520	4	10	354	4
2	218	3	11	164	3
3	380	4	12	420	4
4	382	4	13	407	4
5	532	5	14	305	4
6	398	4	15	555	5
7	516	4	16	365	4
8	203	3	17	508	4
9	521	5	18	663	5
Out	3,670	36	In	3,741	37
			Total	7,411	73

into the wind and even the world's best professionals only manage an average drive on this hole of 232 yards/212 m. Compare this with the downhill, downwind 18th on which they drive an average of 356 yards/326 m.

In a way, such statistics distort the true values of the course. These are no circus-trick holes, but thought-provoking, beautifully crafted gems that respond to thoughtful play. The 6th is a good example. Its fairway is wonderfully wide and inviting, but to have the easiest access to the green you must take the most daring line off the tee, to the right, risking perishing down the cliffs on that side, yet using the wind from the right to coax the ball on to the fairway.

The 6th is followed by another simple but strategic hole, with a wide fairway, requiring you to hold the ball on the left-to-right slope to gain the best line into the green. And, traditionalists that they are, Coore and Crenshaw constructed the approach to the green in such a way as to encourage the old-fashioned bump-and-run shot. Here the golf is as inspiring as the magnificent views.

Kiawah Island

Ocean Course, Kiawah Island Golf Resort, South Carolina, U.S.A.

Never has a name rung so true as "The Ocean Course," for the Atlantic Ocean is in view on every single hole. Ten holes are directly on the coast, the greatest number of seaside holes on any course in the northern hemisphere, and the other eight play parallel to them. This remarkable feature not only provides some of the most scenic golf imaginable, but also makes the course massively affected by the wind. Interestingly, as with the 17th at Sawgrass, this trademark was not intended by the designer Pete Dye, who had planned to sit the course behind the dunes until his wife Alice suggested raising the course in order to provide the stunning sea views.

The unbelievable beauty of the course disguises its brutal difficulty. Dye made use of the natural environment, with dunes and tall grasses devouring poor shots. The most distinctive design feature is that different shot options are always available. Many holes reward daring carries, but players are never forced to take these lines. From the tee and fairway, players must pick a shot to suit their ability and the conditions.

The wide range of options makes for innovative golf, and it is also mandatory on a course so affected by the wind. It has been estimated that wind changes can alter club selection by up to eight clubs, so there needs to be a route for every strength and direction of wind.

Extensive lakes and vast tracts of sandy waste await the inaccurate shot, making this a fine matchplay course but the very devil on which to keep a medal card going.

LEFT *Like the 17th at Sawgrass, Dye wondered if the par-3 17th was dramatic enough, so he added an enormous lake to carry!*

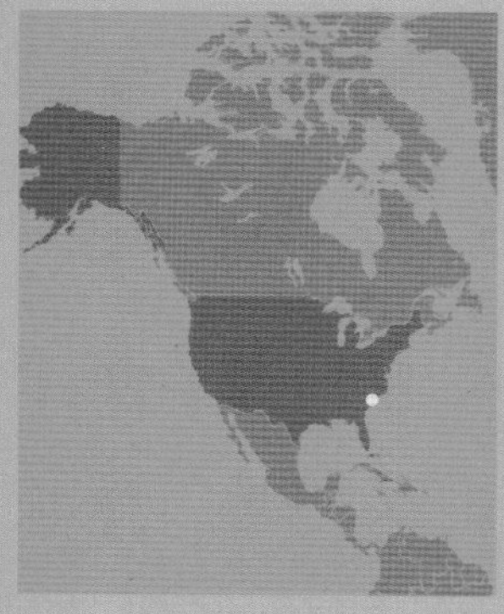

RIGHT *The sand areas are not considered hazards so you may ground your club. This is the par-4 9th hole.*

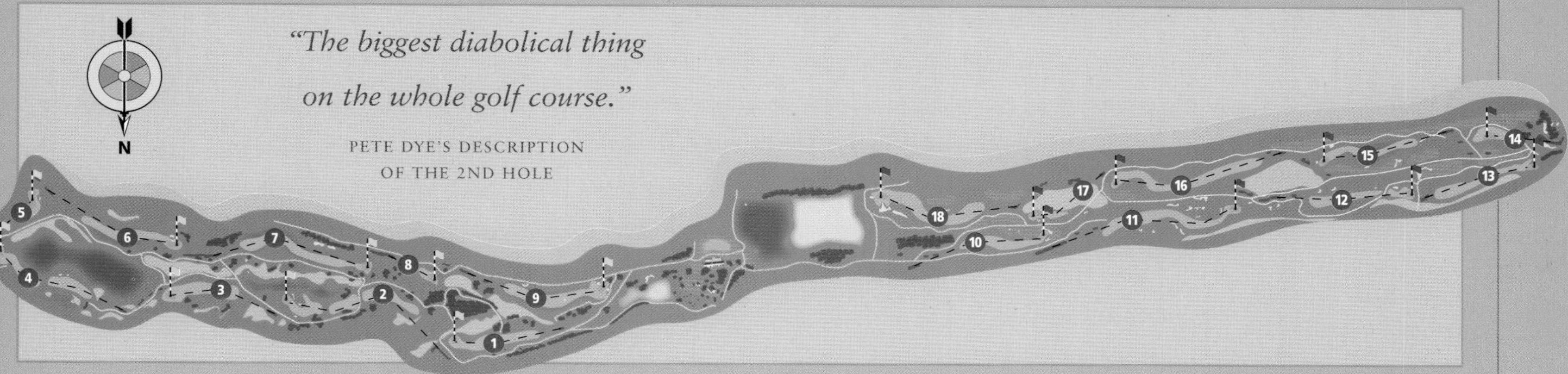

"The biggest diabolical thing on the whole golf course."

PETE DYE'S DESCRIPTION OF THE 2ND HOLE

Creative challenges

The par-5 2nd hole is a good reflection of the course. From the tee, players will be struck by the epic view toward the ocean. But they will also be faced with golfing dilemmas in choosing the correct angle from the tee to cross the marshland that spells golfing disaster if you come up short. A safe shot plays out right for the less bold. If the drive was overly cautious, the second shot must be laid up short of another marsh, 110 yards/101 m in front of the green. Good players should be able to get around the green in two, but that is not the end of the story, as the green is a difficult raised shelf, rolling away into a deep bunker. After a gentle opening hole, the 2nd can be a real nemesis, and even the professionals rack up big scores here. In the 1991 Ryder Cup, Seve Ballesteros won the 2nd with a double-bogey to Wayne Levi's 8!

Like a true links, the options for shot-making are endless, and the longer holes tend to offer a route in on the ground, as well as an airborne approach. You are continually challenged to think hard and pick the right shot. With the design so demanding of creative golf it is no surprise that the Ryder Cup was such a success—the PGA Championship in 2012 should be a real treat.

CARD OF THE COURSE

Hole	Distance (yards)	Par	Hole	Distance (yards)	Par
1	395	4	10	439	4
2	543	5	11	562	5
3	390	4	12	466	4
4	453	4	13	404	4
5	207	3	14	194	3
6	455	4	15	421	4
7	527	5	16	579	5
8	197	3	17	221	3
9	464	4	18	439	4
Out	3,631	36	In	3,725	36
			Total	**7,356**	**72**

Merion

Merion

East Course, Ardmore, Pennsylvania, U.S.A.

"I love Merion. It is one of those old-time golf courses that doesn't have the length of some of the modern-day courses, but still stands the test. That's the mark of a great golf course to me." That was Jack Nicklaus's opinion of Merion East, one of two distinctive courses at this great club in the outskirts of Philadelphia. It held the record for being the shortest course in modern times to host the U.S. Open, which it last did in 1981. Happily, Merion has been reinstated on the U.S. Open roster and will see the return of this great championship in 2013.

BELOW *A ridge crosses the 9th green making the putting surface uphill at the front and back, but downhill in the middle, which Ben Crenshaw described as "very tough to read."*

Merion's golfing beginnings lay, strangely enough, within the members of the Merion Cricket Club. They formed a golf section and laid out a nine-hole course in Haverford, but it soon proved too short and too restrictive for their ambitions. One of their young members, Hugh Wilson, had captained the golf team at Princeton, and in 1910 he was despatched to Britain for seven months to study the architecture of the best courses. Perhaps it is no surprise, then, that there is a feeling of both English heathland and Scottish links about Merion, and the bunkering is every bit as formidable as that on any of the British Open links.

An aura of perfection

The distinguished golf course designer Tom Doak maintains that Merion's East Course is probably the only course that any major golf architect would find it difficult, if not impossible, to improve. That is quite a tribute to Wilson, who had never designed anything before.

Key to survival at Merion is to avoid the bunkers. There are 128 of them and a third of those are encountered in the first three holes. Key to winning at Merion is to overcome the subtleties of the greens, once described by Herbert Warren Wind, the doyen of golf writers, as wonderfully

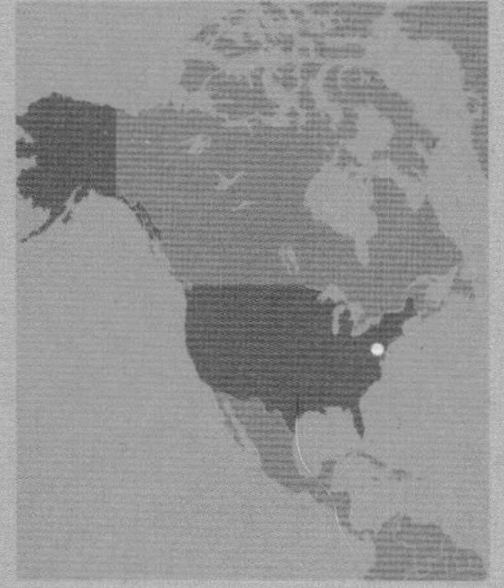

varied, "plateau greens, bench greens, crown greens, sunken greens, large greens, small greens, two-level greens, three-level greens, and greens that slope in a hundred different directions."

One of the most intimidating opening tee shots is encountered at Merion, not because the hole is any more fearsome than the other 17, but because the tee is located right next to a terrace under the awning of which members and their guests take their coffee, lunches, and teas. The consequences of a snap hook are unthinkable! It is, in fact, a fine hole, calling for precise placement of the tee shot to give access to the cleverly angled green.

There are only two par 5s at Merion, but length is largely irrelevant here, guile being of the essence. Take the par-4 11th, for instance. Most of us would have no difficulty steering our tee shot downhill to the nominated landing zone, but the pitch to the green is entirely over deep rough, a stream bounds the green to the right and behind, and the putting surface is small and firm. It was on this famous green that Bob Jones completed his "Impregnable Quardrilateral" in 1930 by winning the U.S. Amateur.

The finish from the 14th is memorable, with the 16th and 17th being played over the remains of an old quarry, and the drive at the 18th formidable, up and over a rock face.

HOGAN'S COURAGE

Ben Hogan played the 1950 U.S. Open at Merion in great pain, having been seriously injured in an automobile crash the previous year. On the 13th hole in the final round he said to his caddie that he could not go on. "I don't work for quitters. I'll see you on the 14th tee, Sir," was his caddie's reply. Hogan labored on, through terrible pain, and forced his way into a three-way play-off (over a further 18 holes) for the title, which he duly won.

CARD OF THE COURSE

Hole	Distance (yards)	Par
1	350	4
2	556	5
3	219	3
4	597	5
5	504	4
6	487	4
7	345	4
8	359	4
9	206	3
Out	3,623	36
10	325	4
11	367	4
12	403	4
13	120	3
14	438	4
15	411	4
16	430	4
17	246	3
18	505	4
In	3,245	34
Total	**6,868**	**70**

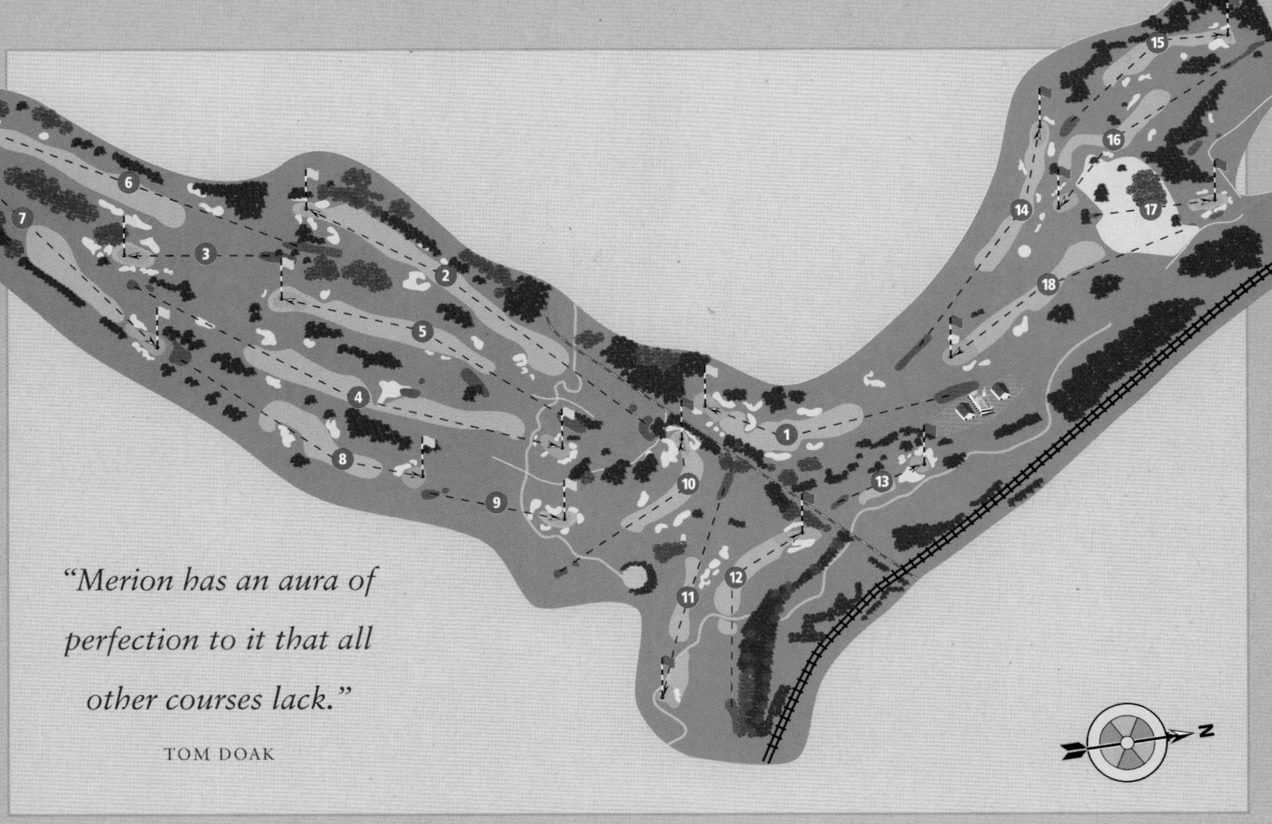

"Merion has an aura of perfection to it that all other courses lack."

TOM DOAK

When Bob Jones won the 1930 U.S. Amateur at Merion, he was never taken beyond the 14th hole. In the 36-hole final, his margin of victory over E. V. Homans was 8 and 7.

Merion's flagsticks are topped not with flags but with wicker baskets, so that the golfer can get no indication of the strength or direction of the wind.

33

Oakmont

Oakmont

Oakmont Country Club, Pennsylvania, U.S.A.

Oakmont is a family course, owing its whole concept and being to Henry Fownes and his son William. Henry was an exceedingly wealthy steel magnate who purchased a large plot of land near Pittsburgh in 1903 with the idea of creating a world-class golf course. William subsequently became one of America's best amateur golfers, winning the 1910 U.S. Amateur Championship and twice playing in the Walker Cup, and was also very influential within the political side of the game. Between them, they created something approaching a golfing behemoth, and had the clout to ensure that it was used for the most prestigious tournaments.

As first built, the course was long but not particularly difficult. It was William who beefed it up in the 1920s, making it so unforgiving that it has been called the toughest course in America. For starters he set about rebunkering the course. At one time there were 220; today about 175 remain. For these Fownes devised a venomous rake: it created golf-ball-sized furrows in the sand, which were drawn across the line of play to make escape almost impossible! And then there were the greens, quite unlike any others, a remarkable assortment of sizes and shapes and, in particular, slopes. To make them the most terrifying greens in the world he had them rolled with huge barrels of sand, insisting that absolutely no watering was done to them.

The greens were also cut phenomenally low—shaved—and with the deep, clinging rough grown in to narrow the fairways for a major tournament the course fully justified its macabre reputation. Today's professionals are used to tricked-up courses with lightning-fast greens, but, with the exception perhaps of Augusta, they rarely play courses with such contours to the greens.

Great design

Surprisingly, Oakmont is not grotesque. It is handsome (more so since the removal of a great many trees that had threatened to choke the course) and strategic, and it responds to thoughtful play. The 3rd hole, for instance, is famed for its Church Pew bunkers—deep sandy trenches separated by rows of treacherous grass ridges—but the greater interest is provided by the green, which is difficult to access, being raised up to repel anything but the truest of approach shots. Miss this green and that's when the scrambling starts.

A glance at the card might suggest that the 17th would be a pushover for today's powerful champions. Not so! It can be driven, but that involves successfully carrying a minefield of bunkers on the left (the direct line from the tee) and somehow managing to squeeze the ball on to the putting surface between another bunker and deceptive low ground to the left. The hole can be played conservatively, but it is dangerously tempting to attack and remarkably resistant to it. And that seems to sum up so much about Oakmont.

LEFT *The famous Church Pew bunkers separating the 3rd and 4th fairways. As can be seen from this photograph, the bunkers to the right of the fairway are hardly less intimidating!*

CARD OF THE COURSE

Hole	Distance (yards)	Par	Hole	Distance (yards)	Par
1	482	4	10	435	4
2	341	4	11	379	4
3	428	4	12	667	5
4	609	5	13	183	3
5	382	4	14	358	4
6	194	3	15	500	4
7	479	4	16	231	3
8	288	3	17	313	4
9	477	4	18	484	4
Out	3,680	35	In	3,550	35
			Total	**7,230**	**70**

Describing Oakmont's one-time bunker rakes, Jimmy Demaret said, "You could have combed North Africa with those and Rommel wouldn't have got past Casablanca."

In 1973 Johnny Miller scored an unbelievable 63 in the last round to win the U.S. Open. It is considered by many to be the greatest round of golf ever played.

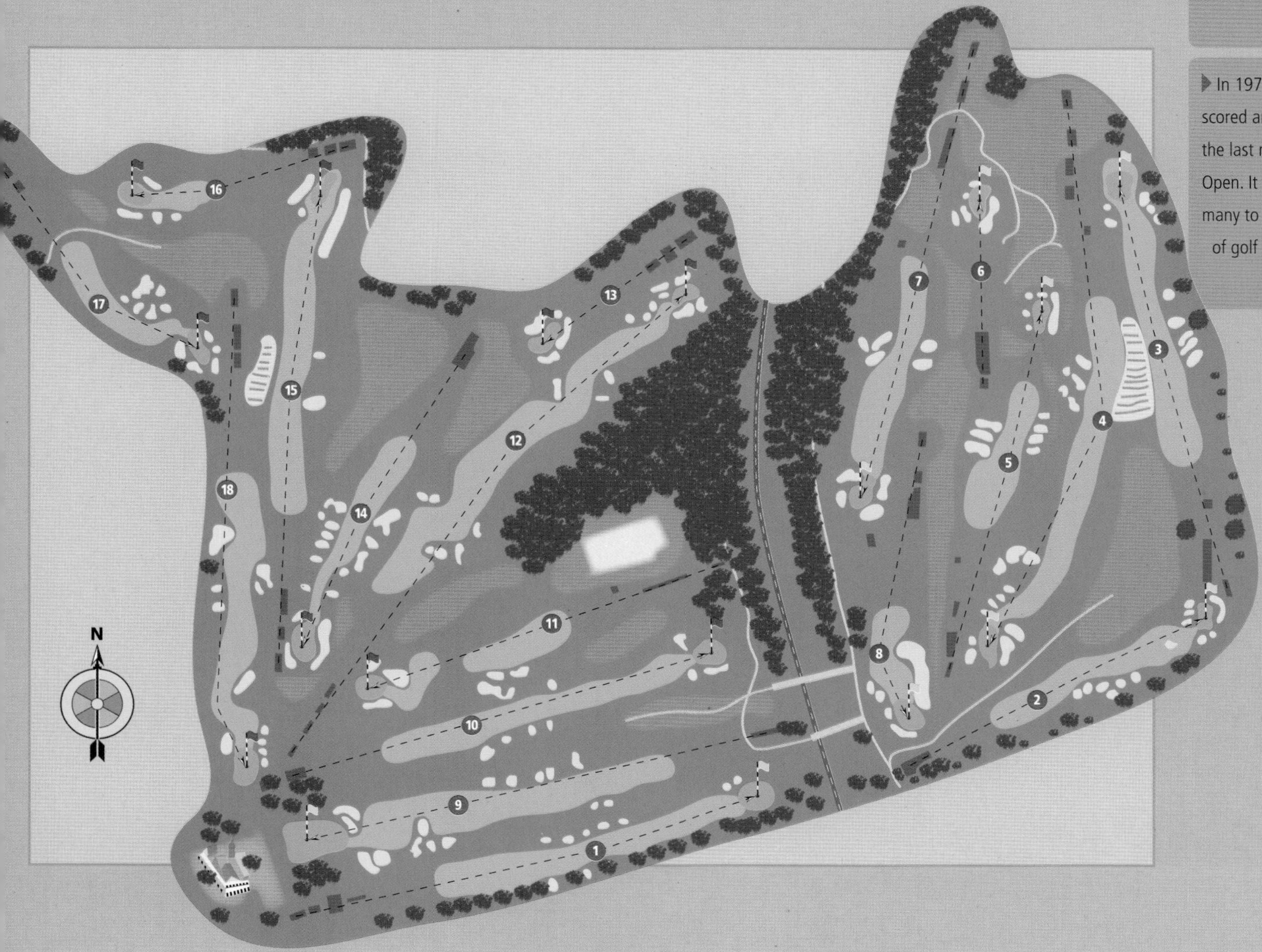

Pebble Beach

Pebble Beach Golf Links, Pebble Beach, California, U.S.A.

Pebble Beach is universally regarded as one of the world's best public courses. It was chosen as the venue for the 100th U.S. Open in 2000, the fourth time it had hosted the Open, yet anybody can simply book a tee time and play on this historic stage. There are, of course, two snags: it is very expensive and you must book long in advance.

Pebble Beach opened in 1919 and ten years later became the first course west of the Mississippi to host the U.S. Amateur Championship. A young Jack Nicklaus capped an impressive amateur career here when he won the 1961 U.S. Amateur. The "Golden Bear" was again victorious when Pebble Beach staged its first U.S. Open in 1972. Despite coming second to Tom Watson in 1982, his affection for Pebble Beach never waned, and eventually he bade farewell to the U.S. Open here in 2000, an emotional Nicklaus poignantly sitting on the fence behind the 18th tee, surveying one of the best finishing holes in golf.

The par-5 18th requires nerves of steel, as the entire hole teeters on the edge of the Pacific. It really should be played as a three-shot hole, often with a 3-wood from the tee. In the 2000 U.S. Open, even the apparently infallible Tiger Woods, who would coast to victory by a margin of 15 shots, managed to pull his tee shot into the sea.

Tom Watson showed the perfect way to play the closing holes at Pebble Beach in the 1982 U.S. Open. With one of golf's most famous chip-ins, he made birdie from the rough on the par-3 17th to claim a one-shot lead over Nicklaus. Sensibly Watson hit a 3-wood for position from the 18th tee and laid up with his second shot in the fairway with a 7-iron to leave himself a short iron approach. Again he played safely, approaching the heart of the green as the pin was tucked in behind the front bunker. From there he finished in style, rolling the 20-ft/6-m putt into the center of the cup for a birdie, birdie finish.

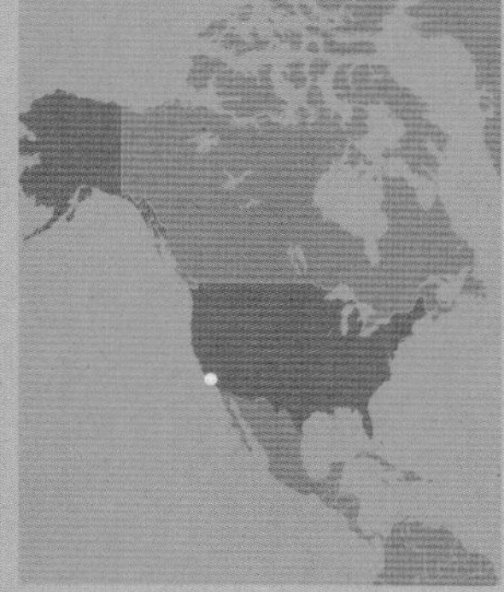

Glorious coastal holes

Stunning holes are abundant here, and from the 4th there is a fabulous sequence of seven consecutive oceanside holes, including the amazing 7th—with wind blowing into your face and the ocean awaiting if you overhit your shot, the prospect from the tee is nerve-racking. The sequence from the 8th to the 10th is one of the greatest trios of consecutive par 4s in world golf. At the 8th, after an exciting drive, you play an awesome approach shot across a corner of the ocean to find the typically small and unreceptive green.

Throughout the round you are presented with daunting drives at undulating fairways, but it is the approach shots where ingenuity is called for. On one hole with wind behind, only a high fade will stop on the tiny green, but on the next you may be playing straight into the wind and having to hit a low punch shot. With a course designed for such inventive golf, and backed by breathtaking views, many golfers would share Jack Nicklaus's view that this is possibly the best course in the world. As Billy Andrade said, "It's the Holy Grail for us."

▶ In 2001 *Golf Digest* ranked Pebble Beach the No.1 course in America , the first time a public course achieved this position. It's a course that everyone wants to play, and it will cost you around $500 to do so.

▶ 17-Mile Drive, which passes through Pebble Beach, is a private toll road. The Pebble Beach Company owns the copyright on all photographic sites on this scenic route—and there are a lot of them!

LEFT *One of the best-known, and most photographed, closing holes in golf, the 18th at Pebble Beach, hugging the Pacific Ocean for every one of its 543 yards/497 m.*

CARD OF THE COURSE

Hole	*Distance (yards)*	*Par*
1	381	4
2	502	5
3	390	4
4	331	4
5	188	3
6	513	5
7	106	3
8	418	4
9	466	4
Out	3,295	36
10	446	4
11	380	4
12	202	3
13	399	4
14	573	5
15	397	4
16	403	4
17	178	3
18	543	5
In	3,521	36
Total	**6,816**	**72**

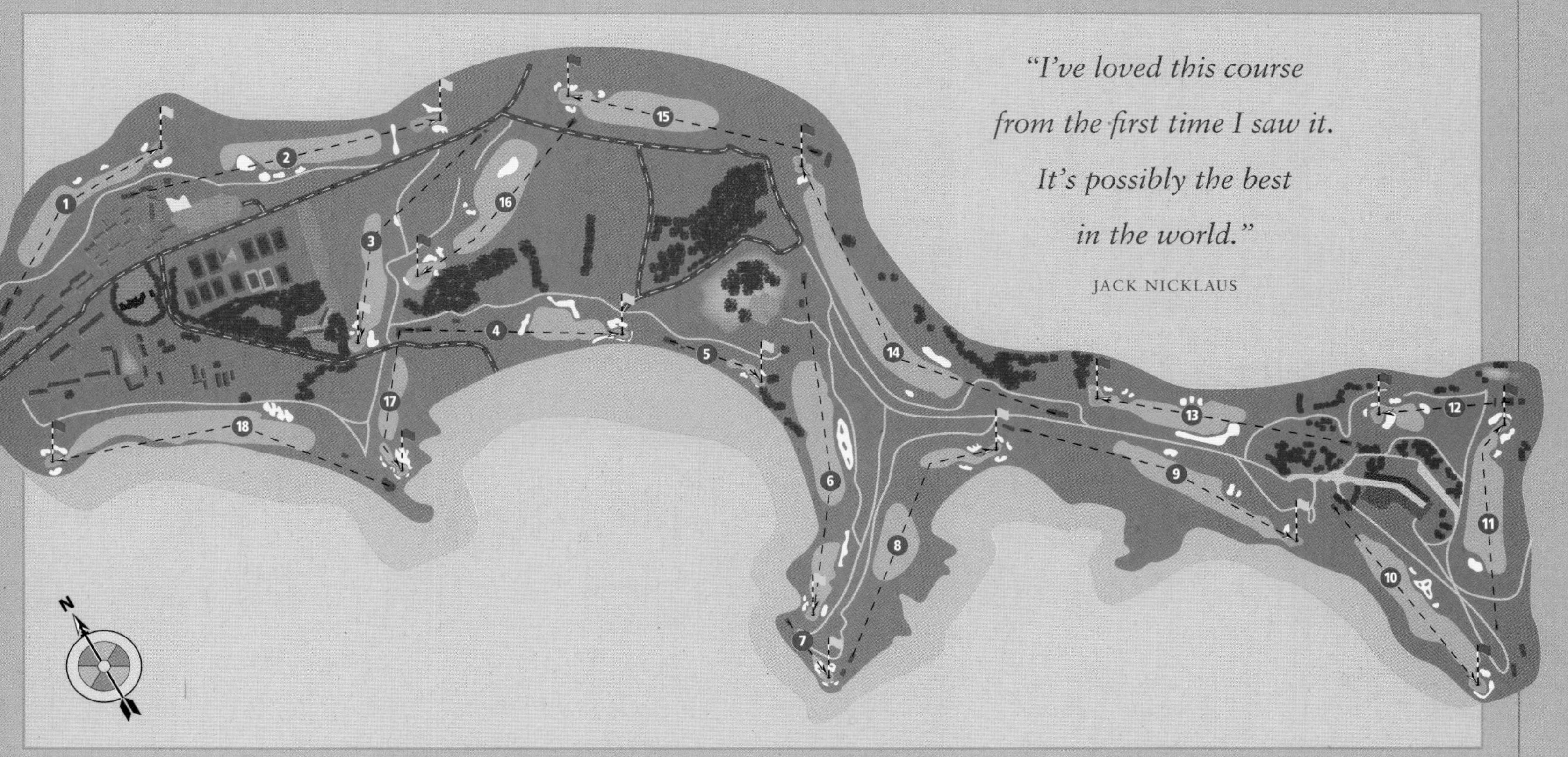

"I've loved this course from the first time I saw it. It's possibly the best in the world."

JACK NICKLAUS

AN IMPRESSIVE QUARTET

The world-famous Pebble Beach Golf Links is but one of four challenging courses at this luxury resort. Spyglass Hill, designed by Robert Trent Jones, is one of the hardest courses on the professional tour. It starts in links-like country beside the ocean before moving inland among woods. The Links at Spanish Bay is one of the few courses in which Tom Watson had a hand in the design (with Robert Trent Jones Jr. and Sandy Tatum). It pays homage to the great Scottish links. Less well-known is the charming Del Monte Golf Course, the oldest course (opened in 1897) in continuous use west of the Mississippi.

ABOVE *It is said that Robert Louis Stevenson walked this shore many times looking for inspiration for* Treasure Island. *This is the 9th tee.*

RIGHT *Bucking the trend that holes need to be outrageously long to be testing, the diminutive 7th is a mere 106 yards/97 m long. Its difficulties are plain to see.*

Pine Valley

Pine Valley

Pine Valley Golf Club, Clementon, New Jersey, U.S.A.

Pine Valley has a reputation for being the hardest course in the world. Yes, the Ocean Course at Kiawah Island might play considerably harder from the back tees in a gale, and many a modern layout, with water on all 18 holes, could be tricked up to be almost unplayable. But, on a daily basis, Pine Valley is the hardest, simply because it asks the golfer to play total golf on every single shot, with the penalty for failure dire. What is so extraordinary about Pine Valley is that no one who has played it would begrudge it a single dropped stroke. It is a masterpiece.

It was a Pittsburgh hotelier, George Crump, a fine amateur player in his own right, who came up with the idea for this course. He had clear views about what he wanted to achieve and for some five years he lived on the site, directing construction. However, he was wise enough to consult others, including Walter Travis and Jerome Travers, two of America's leading amateur golfers in the early years of the 20th century, and the English architect Harry Colt. Quite how much each of them contributed may never be known, but Crump died in 1918 before the course was finished. Today's 12th to 15th holes were completed by Hugh Wilson, the genius of Merion, probably with advice and input from Hugh Alison, Colt's design partner.

Pine Valley today is rather different from the course that was completed in 1919, in that hundreds of thousands of trees have matured to add to the existing perils. Essentially there are tees, narrow strips of grass, which might be called fairways, swathes of sandy waste, and a dense forest—and fiendish greens.

BELOW *The shortest hole at Pine Valley, the 10th, is a wicked little hole. The target is tiny, and missing it is likely to call for miraculous powers of recovery.*

It used to be said that nobody could break 80 on their first visit to Pine Valley. Someone who did was a young Arnold Palmer. He won enough money from bets with the members that he was able to get married!

The ultimate in punitive golf

There are no weak holes at Pine Valley, but three in particular have world renown—the 5th, 7th, and 13th. The 5th is a brutal "short" hole—a full carry of around 230 yards/210 m over a lake and up a hill to a raised green isolated in the woodlands. It would be intimidating at half its length.

Most famous of all the holes is the 7th, a remarkable par 5 made infamous by Hell's Half Acre, a huge expanse of sand splitting the fairway between 285 yards/261 m and 385 yards/352 m from the tee. Get your drive wrong and you cannot clear it with your second. Get the drive right but mishit the second and you are still facing disaster. Get your first and second right and you are left with a devilish pitch to a green entirely surrounded by sand.

BELOW *The 5th hole remains extraordinarily demanding with 21st-century clubs and balls. What it must have been like with those of 1919 hardly bears thinking about.*

It is something similar on the 13th. You drive over a wilderness to an island fairway in the far distance. Then follows a terrifying shot, all carry, of 200 yards/183 m or more over scrub and sand to a green angled away to the left with no margin for error front, back, left, or right. Yet despite the difficulties of each hole there is amazing variety to the course, with welcome change of pace, particularly within the two-shot holes. Hard yes, but still we come back for more.

CARD OF THE COURSE

Hole	*Distance (yards)*	*Par*
1	421	4
2	368	4
3	198	3
4	451	4
5	235	3
6	387	4
7	636	5
8	326	4
9	459	4
Out	3,481	35
10	161	3
11	397	4
12	337	4
13	486	4
14	220	3
15	615	5
16	475	4
17	345	4
18	483	4
In	3,519	35
Total	**7,000**	**70**

Pinehurst

Pinehurst

Pinehurst No. 2, Pinehurst Resort, North Carolina, U.S.A.

Pinehurst No. 2 stands as a pinnacle of classic golf course design in the United States. Because any major changes to the course happened in its infancy and were overseen by its legendary architect, Donald Ross, the holes share a remarkable harmony.

Ross learned his trade from the best, with an apprenticeship under Old Tom Morris at St. Andrews, following a youth spent at Dornoch on Scotland's Sutherland coast. His career took him to the United States, where he was soon employed at Pinehurst. In 1907 Ross's signature course was completed. His affection for it was such that he built himself a house next to the 3rd green. The course evolved under his watchful eye. In 1934 the greens were converted from compressed sand (common in the southern states at that time) to grass, and in 1935 the layout was altered for the last time to roughly its present state.

"Fun golf"

Strange to say, No. 2 has no "signature holes" as such. It is the collection of all 18 holes that makes this a great course. Wide fairways and large greens reflect Ross's links influence, although here the fairways amble through tall pines. The fairway width requires players to target a particular side depending on where the pin is cut. "Turtle back" greens have always been a feature of the course, rolling away poor shots uncompromisingly. In the 1999 U.S. Open, the professionals demonstrated the difficulties, finding just 52 percent of the greens in regulation on the first day.

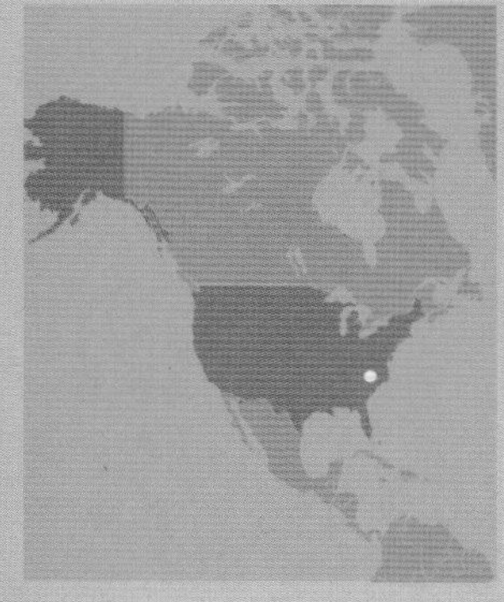

ABOVE *The par 3s on No. 2 are perhaps less celebrated than the par 4s, but they are each handsome, requiring intelligent and subtle play to tame them. This is the 15th.*

LEFT *The daunting approach to the 5th green on Pinehurst No. 2, the putting surface raised up in typical Ross fashion, repelling all but the most truly struck of golf shots.*

Pinehurst has been the venue for a number of great tournaments, but it is the 1999 U.S. Open—one of the hardest-fought championships of all—for which it is best remembered. John Daly fell foul of Ross's design on the final day, as his putt from off the green on the 8th failed to climb the slope, rolling back to his feet. He whacked it away in frustration while it was still moving, eventually putting out for an 11. All the big names were in the hunt at the end, with Woods, Vijay Singh, and Phil Mickelson challenging. After precision golf all week, Payne Stewart needed a putt of 15 feet/5 m on the last to win. "When I looked up, it was about two feet from the hole and breaking right into the center of the cup," he recalled. Stewart was the first person in U.S. Open history to hole a sizable putt on the last to win. A few months later he died in a flying accident.

Woods sums up the attributes of this hundred-year-old design: "I play courses on tour and we all see it—miss the green, atomic lob wedge, hack it out of the rough. That for me is not fun golf. Fun golf is Pinehurst."

CARD OF THE COURSE

Hole	*Distance (yards)*	*Par*
1	405	4
2	472	4
3	384	4
4	568	5
5	476	4
6	224	3
7	407	4
8	467	4
9	190	3
Out	3,593	35
10	611	5
11	478	4
12	451	4
13	380	4
14	471	4
15	206	3
16	510	4
17	190	3
1	445	4
In	3,742	35
Total	**7,335**	**70**

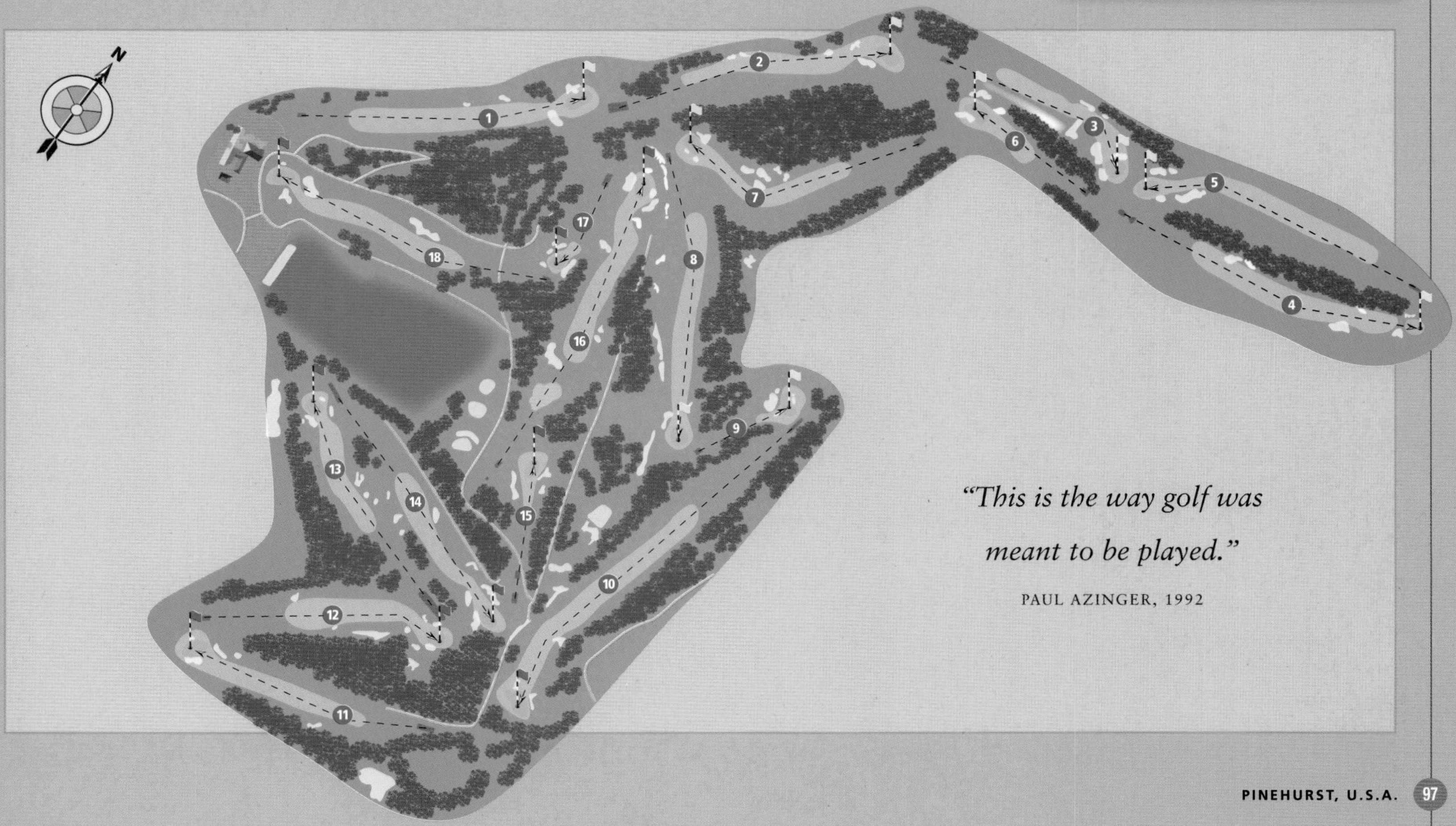

"This is the way golf was meant to be played."

PAUL AZINGER, 1992

Shinnecock Hills

Shinnecock Hills

Shinnecock Hills Golf Club, Southampton, Long Island, New York, U.S.A.

One of the United States' oldest championship courses, Shinnecock Hills was founded in the affluent Hamptons on Long Island back in 1891. By 1896 it was ready to host its first important championships, the U.S. Amateur and U.S. Open, both being held for only the second time. After taking its place at the top of the pecking order, Shinnecock merged into the background for nearly 100 years, its golf being entirely social.

ABOVE *The routing of Shinnecock Hills brings the 9th and 18th holes back in parallel to deliciously sited greens on the slopes beneath the club's splendid clubhouse.*

A new layout followed in 1916, but the club did not seek further public attention. The same happened when the building of a new highway on Long Island forced further changes in 1930–31, a layout ignored for further national championship play until 1986, when the golfing world at large was awakened to the magnificent course that had been hidden from public gaze for so long. The U.S. Open had returned and it was clear that this would not be a one-off affair—there were repeat visits in 1995 and 2004.

To create this long-concealed gem, the club called on William Flynn, an architect who had previously worked mostly in the Philadelphia area. He and his business partner Howard Toomey are now recognized as one of the most imaginative partnerships in what was a particularly creative era of American golf design, between the two World Wars. In fact Flynn retained two holes from the previous course (designed by Charles Blair Macdonald and Seth Raynor, another great partnership) but the rest was brand new.

▶ Shinnecock's clubhouse, designed in 1892 by fashionable architect Stanford White (whose womanizing led to his murder in 1906), was the first purpose-built clubhouse in the United States and is still in use today.

A genuine links?

Shinnecock Hills has been described as the nearest America gets to a true links, as exemplified by Britain's ancient links. Is this so? The answer has to be "No" on two counts. First, there are "inland links" far from the sea, such as Sand Hills in Nebraska, which play more like the Old Course than Shinnecock ever can. Second, the sea is not really a factor in how play is made, how the shots must be shaped, as it is (if often indirectly) on a true links. And yet, in so many ways, Shinnecock reminds us of a links. Its wide spaces are windswept, and the direction of the wind is often hugely important in how the play of an individual hole might change from day to day, or hour to hour. And Shinnecock is far hillier than Dornoch, Royal Aberdeen and St. Andrews thrown together.

It would be invidious to single out any particular hole at Shinnecock because it is the collective strength of all 18 holes that makes this such an outstanding course. It might be by far the shortest of recent U.S. Open courses, but part of its strength is the way the course is maintained, with firm-and-fast conditioning demanding great skill in approach work allied to formidable rough—the sort of thing the R&A conjured up for the infamous 1999 British Open at Carnoustie. At Shinnecock that is normal!

This is, in golfing terms, a favored corner of Long Island, with the famous National Golf Links literally next door and the Jack Nicklaus/Tom Doak Sebonack adjoining that.

CARD OF THE COURSE

Hole	*Distance (yards)*	*Par*
1	393	4
2	226	3
3	478	4
4	435	4
5	537	5
6	474	4
7	189	3
8	398	4
9	443	4
Out	3,573	35
10	412	4
11	158	3
12	468	4
13	370	4
14	443	4
15	403	4
16	540	5
17	179	3
18	450	4
In	3,423	35
Total	**6,996**	**70**

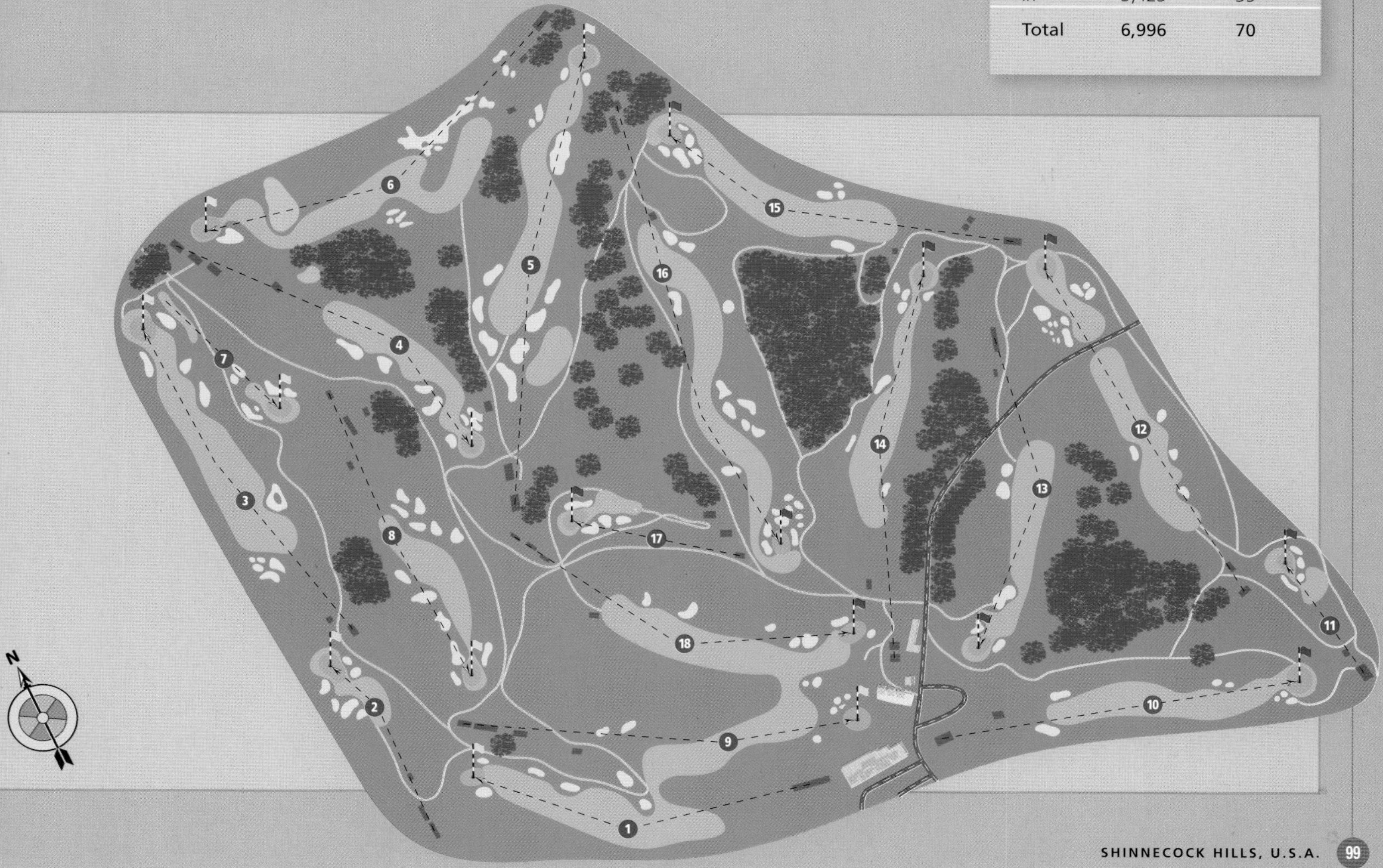

Torrey Pines

South Course, Torrey Pines, San Diego, California, U.S.A.

Named after the indigenous trees that dot the fairways, the two courses at Torrey Pines occupy a remarkable location, perched atop high cliffs that fall steeply into the Pacific Ocean. There are exceptional views from the courses. Both courses—North and South—are of high quality, and when the annual Buick Invitational is played, for the first two days play is divided between the two courses with one round played on each. For the weekend, however, all rounds are played on the South Course.

In 2001, Rees Jones renovated the South Course at a cost of $3.5 million, which saw the holes lengthened to a staggering 7,607 yards/6,956 m. At 483 yards/442 m, the 4th is a long, unforgiving par 4, with two bunkers lurking down the right fairway. But players' eyes are inevitably drawn left to the stunning view of pine trees marking the edge of land and the beginning of the Pacific. As with most of the tee shots, the fairway is actually played to at a slight angle, and this brings its own difficulties in finding the short grass from the tee. Tucked among the trees and protected by a large bunker, the heart-shaped green appears very small when approached by the long-iron or wood of most players.

Like so many great courses, the South Course also finishes well, with a decision-making par 5. Bunkers left and right narrow the fairway landing area, but a straight shot leaves the potential to attack the green in two. With a substantial water hazard in front of the left-hand side of the green, many players inevitably lay up. Undoubtedly, it is a dramatic finishing hole for the 2008 U.S. Open, the first major to be played here.

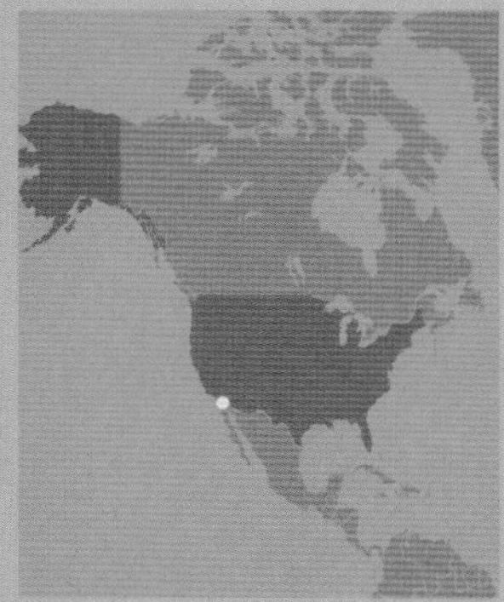

▶ The city of San Diego owns these municipal courses, and anybody can line up and get a starting time. The only problem is that the wait starts from as early as 6 p.m. the night before!

LEFT *The 12th is the toughest hole on the South Course, a long par 4 with a tightly protected raised green. The view over the Pacific Ocean is incomparable.*

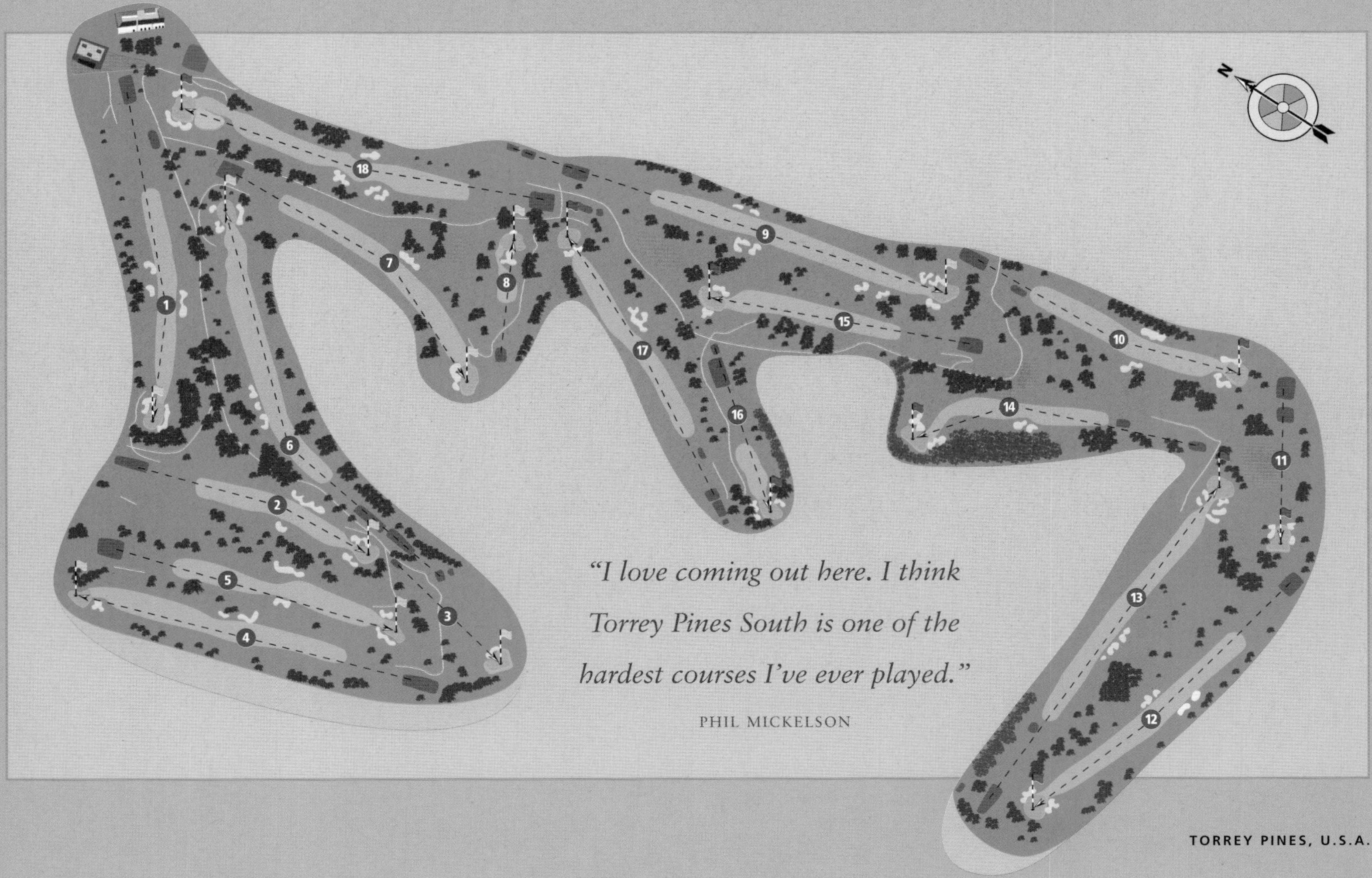

Tiger's winning streak

Though the length might be intimidating for most players, the longest course in regular PGA tournament play must seem fairly simple to Tiger Woods, who tamed the brutal course with a final-round 66 to win the Buick Invitational in 2007. In an awesome finale, Woods overcame his two-shot deficit in the first two holes and displayed the power and finesse necessary for success at Torrey Pines by lashing a 3-wood 265 yards/242 m to reach the par-5 9th, and rolling in the 25-foot/8-m eagle putt. His victory earned him his fifth Buick title; it was his seventh consecutive PGA win in 2007. He added an astonishing sixth Buick the following year.

Despite the more prestigious tournament pedigree of the South Course, many golfers prefer the slightly easier North Course. Occupying an even more scenic setting, the North Course is shorter, at 6,874 yards/6,286 m, and presents golfers with more tactical challenges of placement and planning as opposed to the sheer brute force of its southern neighbour. The combination of the two courses makes Torrey Pines one of the best and most spectacular municipals in the world.

CARD OF THE COURSE

Hole	*Distance (yards)*	*Par*	*Hole*	*Distance (yards)*	*Par*
1	452	4	10	405	4
2	387	4	11	221	3
3	198	3	12	504	4
4	483	4	13	541	5
5	453	4	14	435	4
6	560	5	15	477	4
7	462	4	16	227	3
8	176	3	17	442	4
9	613	5	18	571	5
Out	3,784	36	In	3,823	36
			Total	**7,607**	**72**

▶ Torrey Pines is only the second municipal course (after Bethpage Black) to host the U.S. Open. The USGA is demonstrably keen to spread its gospel ever wider.

"I love coming out here. I think Torrey Pines South is one of the hardest courses I've ever played."

PHIL MICKELSON

TPC Sawgrass

TPC Sawgrass

Stadium Course, TPC Sawgrass, Ponte Vedra Beach, Florida, U.S.A.

When the two-year-old course hosted its first tournament, the Players Championship of 1982, the professionals were almost unanimous in their verdict: they hated it! Although the design had always aimed to be tough, clearly it was too much, and Pete Dye, the renowned U.S. golf course designer, modified the course slightly to soften the greens and change particularly brutal bunkers. The changes worked and the Players Championship has now become the unofficial fifth major.

The professionals' opinions were especially important at Sawgrass as TPC (Tournament Players Club) courses are owned by the PGA (Professional Golfers' Association) for the purpose of hosting tournaments. The course is respected by the professionals, as the clever design does not favor a specific type of player. Long hitters like Davis Love and Tiger Woods have won the Players Championship, but so have those relying on accuracy such as Hal Sutton, Justin Leonard, and Tom Kite. Adam Scott won at the age of 23; the following year Fred Funk won aged 48.

The island green

The PGA ownership is reflected in the design, in that the course was created for tournament golf. Huge amounts of earth were removed from the site and used to create spectator mounds surrounding the fairways and greens, the deep holes left from excavation being filled with water, creating plentiful lakes. Such is the fame of the island-green 17th, one of golf's most feared short holes, that an American sports channel devotes itself to showing uninterrupted coverage of the hole during the Players Championship. Interestingly, Dye never intended the 17th green to be surrounded by water. He was planning to make it a giant bunker until his wife suggested the island.

Water comes into play on most holes, notably on the brutal 18th. With a lake on the left of this tough dogleg, players are faced with a "bite off as much as you can chew" concept from the tee. If the drive is not perfectly placed you must lay up the approach, as an aggressive second shot, especially from the clingy rough, tends to be water bound.

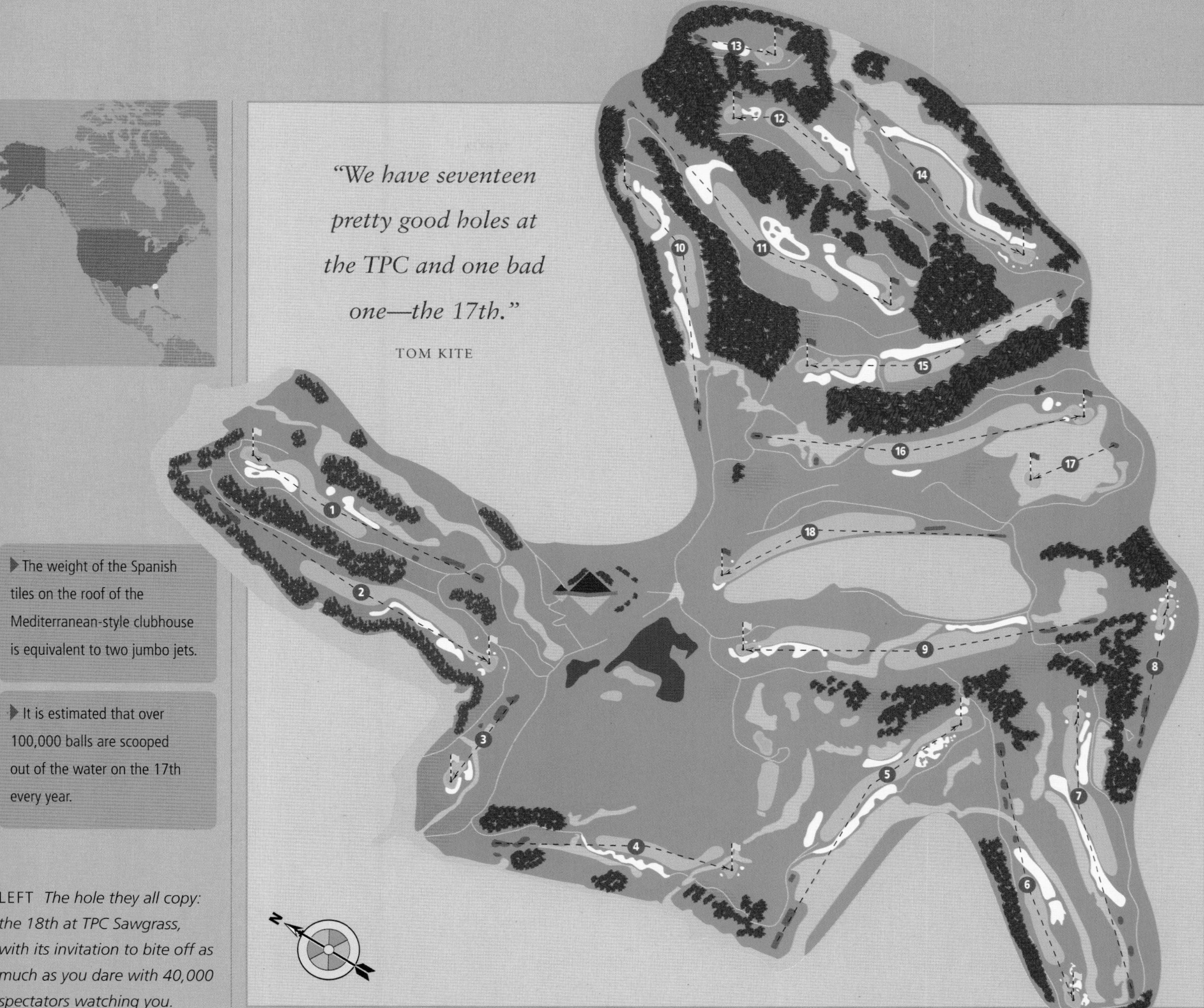

"We have seventeen pretty good holes at the TPC and one bad one—the 17th."

TOM KITE

▶ The weight of the Spanish tiles on the roof of the Mediterranean-style clubhouse is equivalent to two jumbo jets.

▶ It is estimated that over 100,000 balls are scooped out of the water on the 17th every year.

LEFT *The hole they all copy: the 18th at TPC Sawgrass, with its invitation to bite off as much as you dare with 40,000 spectators watching you.*

CARD OF THE COURSE

Hole	Distance (yards)	Par	Hole	Distance (yards)	Par
1	392	4	10	424	4
2	532	5	11	535	5
3	177	3	12	358	4
4	384	4	13	181	3
5	466	4	14	467	4
6	393	4	15	449	4
7	442	4	16	507	5
8	219	3	17	137	3
9	583	5	18	447	4
Out	3,588	36	In	3,505	36
			Total	7,093	72

You don't have to hold your breath for the course to kick in on the 17th. One of the best holes is the reachable par-5 2nd. With palm trees lining the fairway an accurate draw is required from the tee. The hole is deliberately kept at a realistic length so that it is hittable in two, but the second shot is played to one of Dye's trademark small greens, with penalizing rough and pot bunkers offering ample protection.

Recent alterations to the course have emphasized the "hard and fast" style of the design. The result of this is that a wayward shot now has even more chance of running away into trouble, which has been increased through the addition of 200 newly planted trees. The length of the course has changed little since it was first built, only about 200 yards/183 m having been added in nearly 30 years. The emphasis, then, is on creating exciting golf through reachable distances—refreshing in an era when too many other courses are put on steroids for tour events! The biggest change is a new clubhouse in the "stately home" style.

ABOVE AND RIGHT *The 17th hole has acquired a notoriety all of its own. On the opening day of the Players Championship in 1984 no fewer than 64 balls were hit into the water under blustery conditions. The stroke average was 3.79, making it the hardest par 3 in Tour history to that date.*

TPC Scottsdale

TPC Scottsdale

Stadium Course, TPC Scottsdale, Arizona, U.S.A.

Exhilarating golf is abundant when the Tour comes to Scottsdale for the FBR (formerly Phoenix) Open, with the quality of the course playing its part along with the 500,000 fans who make this golf's largest spectator event. The permanent earth galleries around the greens remind one that this is a TPC and, like Sawgrass, it was designed to host PGA events.

Scottsdale has seen many memorable moments, including the famous double-eagle described on the right, Tiger Woods's more conventional hole-in-one on the signature par-3 16th, and Mark Calcavecchia's record 28-under-par tournament total in the 2001 Phoenix Open. Evidently the Weiskopf/Morrish design—commissioned to test the best in Phoenix Open week while allowing fee-paying amateurs who play it the rest of the year a none-too-humbling experience—brings the best out of golfers. It is hard to believe that Scottsdale was one of the first collaborations between the former Open champion Tom Weiskopf and architect Jay Morrish, because the course flows so well. But, then again, this was one of the best design teams of its era.

DOUBLE EAGLE

One of the most memorable shots of tournament golf was played at Scottsdale. On the par-4 17th, Andrew Magee decided to take the water and bunkers out of play by attempting to drive the green. Forgetting to check that the match ahead had left the green, he successfully drove the green, whereupon his ball struck the putter of a surprised Tom Byrum, who was lining up his putt. Byrum was even more surprised to see Magee's ball deflected straight into the hole. It is the only double-eagle scored on a par 4 in PGA Tour history.

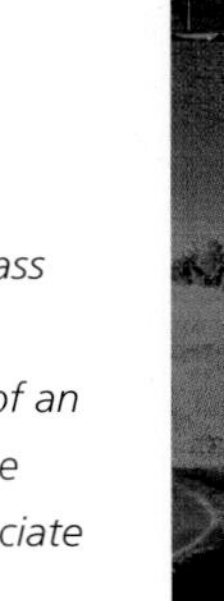

RIGHT *With its green grass and plentiful water TPC Scottsdale is reminiscent of an oasis. It is popular with the professionals, who appreciate its fairness.*

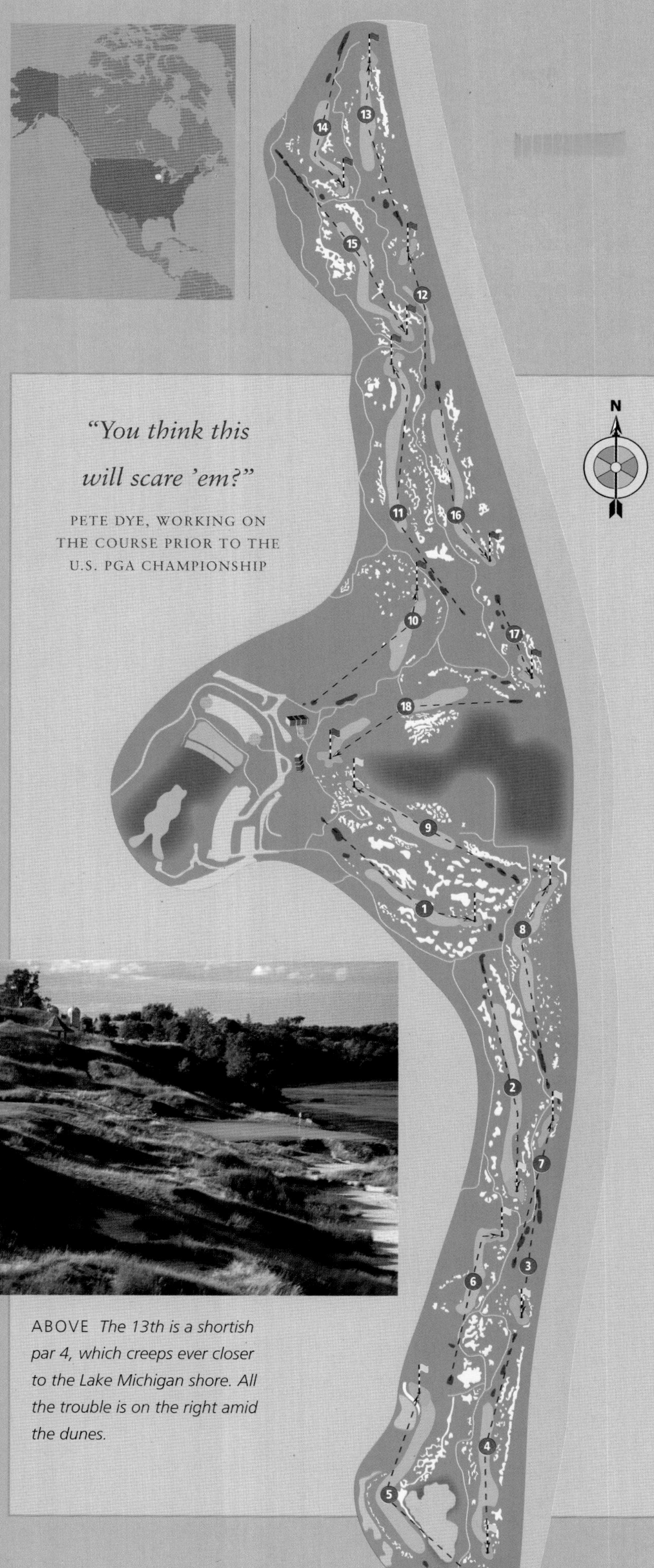

"You think this will scare 'em?"

PETE DYE, WORKING ON THE COURSE PRIOR TO THE U.S. PGA CHAMPIONSHIP

ABOVE *The 13th is a shortish par 4, which creeps ever closer to the Lake Michigan shore. All the trouble is on the right amid the dunes.*

CARD OF THE COURSE

Hole	Distance (yards)	Par	Hole	Distance (yards)	Par
1	405	4	10	389	4
2	592	5	11	619	5
3	183	3	12	166	3
4	455	4	13	403	4
5	584	5	14	372	4
6	391	4	15	465	4
7	214	3	16	535	5
8	462	4	17	223	3
9	415	4	18	489	4
Out	3,701	36	In	3,661	36
			Total	7,362	72

On the shores of Lake Michigan

With 36 superb inland holes established in Kohler's American Club Resort, the plumbing magnate acquired an abandoned army base on the shoreline of Lake Michigan, 9 miles/14 km from his village, and requested the help of Pete Dye to create a traditional links. Having completed massive earthmoving operations in the past, Dye was unperturbed by the drearily flat land, and began the lengthy process of creating the dunes and character of a true links. The result was Whistling Straits, two courses of exceptional charm. Located just inland from the lake, the Irish Course features beautifully mounded fairways surrounded by wispy rough. Incorporated into the traditional links style are four streams to give the course a pleasing variety, with water hazards more associated with parkland.

Most acclaimed of all is the Straits Course. Though the holes may be intimidating, the clever design, including eight waterfront holes, makes this a magnificent place. The 4th hole, named Glory, is truly spectacular, a daunting par 4, with a fairway that kicks left toward the dunes on the edge of Lake Michigan. A long iron is needed to approach the raised green, which sits above devastating bunkers backed by a perfect view of the lake. The 17th is known as Pinched Nerve, which accurately describes one of Dye's most intimidating par 3s of all—and he has designed some very tough ones indeed.

This visually stunning course is creatively designed for interesting golf, but do not pay too much attention to your score—nobody plays to handicap here!

Winged Foot

Winged Foot

West Course, Winged Foot Golf Club, Mamaroneck, New York, U.S.A.

The winged foot is the emblem of the New York Athletic Club, a group of whose members founded the golf club of the same name in 1923. Given that Winged Foot is one of New York's premier clubs, located just off the I-95 New England Thruway, and no more than half an hour from central Manhattan, you might expect the place to be noisy, bustling, and full to the brim with golfers on every hole. Nothing could be further from the truth.

For a start, Winged Foot has two courses: the West, which is the championship course, and the East, which is pretty much its equal. The clubhouse is palatial, and the members know how to relax on a golf course. And yet they do not dawdle on the round. The club expects matches to take no longer than four hours, even in tournaments.

Both courses were laid out by Alfred Tillinghast, an architect of considerable lasting fame in the United States, with Baltusrol, Baltimore, and Bethpage State Park sharing with Winged Foot the honor of hosting U.S. Open Championships. The founding members wanted "a man-sized course," and they got it. What "Tilly" had to work with was largely flat parkland—not, you might think, the most promising canvas. But surely the sign of a great architect is to be able to produce a great course despite the lack of helpful topography, and here he produced two great courses.

RIGHT *Tillinghast's short holes are a study in themselves, so often imaginatively created from unpromising terrain. The 10th at Winged Foot West is one of his absolute best*

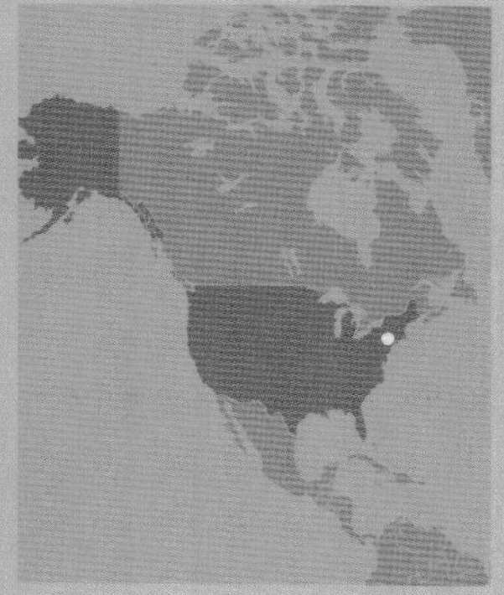

▶ During the 2006 U.S. Open the 1st and 18th were the joint most difficult holes against par, both averaging 4.471. The only hole to have an average score below par was the par-5 5th, which averaged 4.654.

▶ Winged Foot may look natural to the eye, but it was actually created by blasting 7,200 tons of rock and felling 7,800 trees. It took a workforce of 200, with 60 teams of horses and 19 tractors, to complete the task.

Tillinghast's masterly greens

"If it has not got anything about it that might make it respectable, it has got to have quality knocked into it until it can hold its head up in polite society," was Tillinghast's philosophy, and the quality he knocked into Winged Foot was particularly on and around the greens. They are nearly all raised up above the generally flat fairways, mischievously contoured and punishingly bunkered. Fortunately Tillinghast's design blueprints survive (he worked in minute detail) and to their credit the club has been able to restore the greens to their original size and contours.

Even from the members' tees Winged Foot West is long. Unless you can drive a good distance you will find yourself banging away with wooden-club approaches and if you are not devilishly straight you must surely tangle with the defensive bunkers or lack the control necessary to get the ball close to the pin on these tough greens. And when there is a shorter par 4, such as the 6th, the entrance to the green is incredibly narrow, with the putting surface seriously canted and hidden behind a right-hand protective bunker.

There are moments of respite on the short holes, but, again, only if you can find a way past the narrow entrances and guardian bunkers. Each of the greens is raised sufficiently to reject the shot that is not quite good enough. One of those short holes, the 10th, is world class, played across a valley to a plateau green loyally attended by punitive bunkers. A bewildering putting surface awaits if you do make it safely on to the green. Such is the genius of Tillinghast, whose courses should be on every golfer's wishlist!

CARD OF THE COURSE

Hole	*Distance (yards)*	*Par*
1	450	4
2	453	4
3	216	3
4	469	4
5	515	5
6	321	4
7	162	3
8	475	4
9	514	4
Out	3,575	35
10	188	3
11	396	4
12	640	5
13	214	3
14	458	4
15	416	4
16	478	4
17	449	4
18	450	4
In	3,689	35
Total	**7,264**	**70**

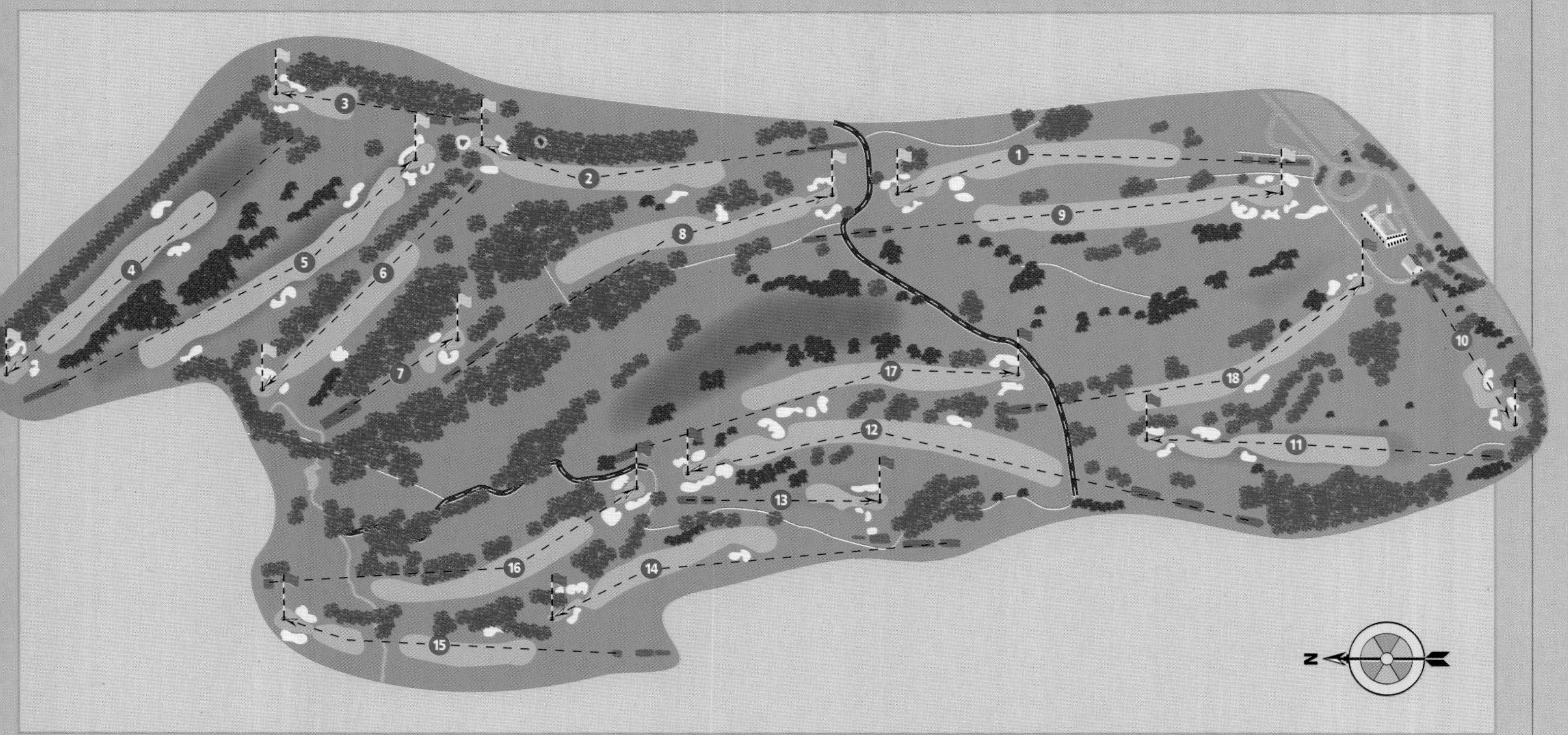

Banff Springs

Banff Springs

Stanley Thompson 18, Fairmont Banff Springs Hotel, Banff, Alberta, Canada

Early golf courses simply evolved. Golfers found a route through whatever natural obstacles they found where they had chosen to play. There was minimal earthmoving. The emergence of the earliest course architects, such as Old Tom Morris, toward the end of the 19th century was accompanied by earthmoving on a very small scale—as much as a couple of men with shovels or possibly with a horse and scraper could move. Enter the steam shovel. It could hardly move mountains, but it could shift a large amount of dirt in a day. Throw in dynamite and almost anything became possible, or it did if you had a huge budget.

The enormous Banff Springs Hotel belonged to the Canadian Pacific Railway (CPR). It was the jewel in their crown, standing proudly overlooking the Spray and Bow Rivers surrounded by the stunning scenery of the Rocky Mountains. It had had a golf course of sorts since 1911, but it hardly matched up to the rest of the facilities on offer at this world-class hotel. The CPR had money and they also had railroad trucks, trainloads of them. They had seen what Canadian architect Stanley Thompson had achieved at their rival railroad Canadian National's resort at Jasper Park, so they hired Thompson themselves.

LUCKY ACCIDENT

Banff's most famous hole, the 4th, Devil's Cauldron, was not part of Thompson's original plan. He had no intention of using this area of the extensive property. However, during the winter of 1927, when heavy snows and bitter temperatures had halted construction work, an avalanche created a new glacial lake. When Thompson returned to Banff he spotted the lake and its potential as the basis for a world-class short hole immediately.

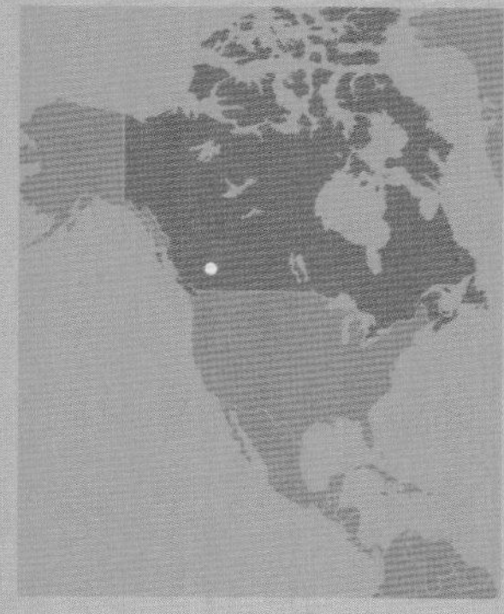

> Because it is too remote from major centers of population Banff Springs has never hosted an important professional tournament.

> Banff Springs is in the middle of a vast national park. Deer are frequently found on the course, and bears are occasional visitors.

LEFT AND BELOW
Wonderful golf in an exquisite setting. Stanley Thompson's course at Banff Springs is exceptional—the 4th hole is, quite simply, one of the greatest holes in golf.

The world's most expensive golf course

It took Thompson and his team two years to build the Banff course, and when it opened in 1929 it was said to be the most expensive course ever built. The great thing about the course is that you would never guess that Thompson had spent so much money and moved so many thousands of tons of earth, for it all looks so natural. And what the unsuspecting eye might not notice is that a lot of Thompson's creativity went into ensuring that manufactured features, such as bunkers, raised greens, and mounds, were perfectly scaled to the grandeur of the surrounding forests and mountains. As a result of such empathy, the course is not overwhelmed by the scenery.

In recent years a new clubhouse has been erected and the original order of playing the holes abandoned. So the course now starts with a hole that throws the golfer straight into the forests. The next two holes turn to face Mount Rundle. Thompson needed dynamite to blast away enough room to build the 3rd fairway. Further dynamite was required to clear the site for the 4th green, but it was well worth it, for the 4th is a world-class short hole (so good that *Golf Magazine* ranks it in the top four in the world), calling for a drop-shot down over a glacial lake to find a well-bunkered green on the far side. After three more holes in the forests the course emerges for a sequence of beautiful holes alongside the Bow River.

Thompson's original opening hole is now the 15th, and many an experienced golfer has stood on that tee and been knocked off their game by the sight ahead, with the sparkling Spray River far below and the tree-lined and bunker-strewn fairway uncomfortably distant on its far side.

CARD OF THE COURSE

Hole	*Distance (yards)*	*Par*
1	415	4
2	180	3
3	535	5
4	200	3
5	430	4
6	380	4
7	610	5
8	160	3
9	510	5
Out	3,420	36
10	225	3
11	425	4
12	450	4
13	230	3
14	445	4
15	480	4
16	420	4
17	385	4
18	585	5
In	3,645	35
Total	**7,065**	**71**

"It's out of this world."

BOBBY LOCKE, THE GREAT SOUTH AFRICAN GOLFER

Highlands Links

Highlands Links Golf Course, Ingonish Beach, Cape Breton, Nova Scotia, Canada

This extraordinarily beautiful golf course had its origins in the aftermath of the Great Depression. The Canadian government wanted to kick-start tourism on this stretch of the Atlantic coast and having observed how successful Stanley Thompson's courses at Jasper Park and Banff Springs had been in boosting the fortunes of both resorts, it seemed sensible to see what he could do at Cape Breton. He would have nothing like the extravagant budget available to him at Banff, but the site had such enormous potential that Thompson leaped at the chance.

ABOVE *The fabulous, and inviting, view from the 6th tee, calling for a long and accurate drive to find the far-distant fairway on this excellent hole.*

Thompson's masters wanted a course that made the most of the sea shore. Thompson, on the other hand, felt that there were, indeed, good holes there, but that an even better course could be made by taking the course inland through the woods and hills of the beautiful Clyburn River valley. Thompson got his way and plenty of manpower to create his course. We can only be thankful that those charged with setting up this course listened to sense and that those who now conserve it do so with understanding.

Enjoy the views

The first six holes keep close company with the Atlantic, giving magnificent seascapes from the higher ground. In fact the opening hole climbs sufficiently to make it a bogey 5 for most of us, but the reward is a long, helpful descent on the 2nd. Already it is apparent that these are some of the bumpiest fairways to be found on a golf course. It is not entirely accidental, for Thompson was a great admirer of Scottish links golf and he used the natural contours of the

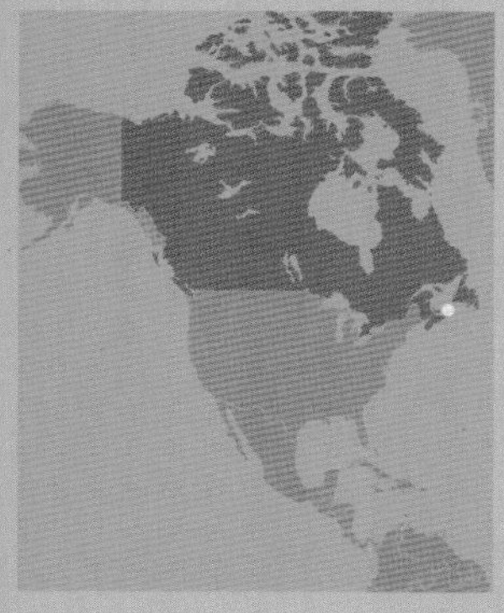

BELOW *Stanley Thompson's genius was not only to route a course to make the most of gorgeous views such as this, the 15th, but to create great holes to indulge them.*

land tellingly—when he could. He also helped to create them artificially, by burying piles of stones and rocks and covering them with grass. This may sound crude, but Thompson was an artist.

Continuing along the coastal stretch of the course, two short holes frame a tempting, but treacherous, short two-shot hole, before the final hole in this section—the first-rate par-5 6th, which is particularly exciting from the championship tee with its 220-yard/201-m carry diagonally over water simply to find the fairway. A walk over the Clyburn River takes us up into the woods for the next par 5, which tumbles down, corkscrewing as it goes to a delightful green at the bottom of the hill. It is a superb hole technically, but even if it were an average hole it would still be ravishing, so glorious is the scenery. So it goes on, fascinating hole after fascinating hole, and so good is it that we forgive Thompson for giving us a long walk, almost a route march from the 12th green to the 13th tee, for it is a lovely walk in its own right.

There is, still to come, a truly breathtaking hole—the 15th. In golfing terms it's a wonderfully stimulating par 5, tempting all of us to have a crack at the green in two, downhill through a jumble of humps, bumps, and sidehill lies. Yet this is played out against the backdrop of the Atlantic Ocean, restored to us after our woodland playground, with the fairway perfectly aligned on Whale Island. Had the fairway and green been a few feet to either side this would have been a good hole. Placed where it is it really does take your breath away.

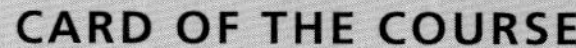

CARD OF THE COURSE

Hole	Distance (yards)	Par
1	405	4
2	447	4
3	160	3
4	324	4
5	164	3
6	537	5
7	570	5
8	319	4
9	336	4
Out	3,262	36
10	145	3
11	512	5
12	240	3
13	435	4
14	398	4
15	540	5
16	460	5
17	190	3
18	410	4
In	3,330	36
Total	**6,592**	**72**

The holes at Highlands Links all have fanciful names with Scottish connections. The short 10th, for instance, is called Cuddy's Lugs, because the bunkers either side of the green reminded Thompson of a donkey's ears.

St. George's

St. George's

St. George's Golf and Country Club, Etobicoke, Ontario, Canada

Stanley Thompson must have known he was on to something good when he was given 2,000 acres/809 ha of rolling hills and meandering rivers from which to plan a course in the new Humber Valley Village. Built in the 1920s, this planned community was designed to resemble an English village, and required a fitting golf course to attract people to the area. With such an enormous expanse of land at his disposal, Thompson was able to decide upon an almost perfect stretch of golfing terrain.

Tall trees, rivers, and an undulating landscape all helped to capture the essence of the best English parkland courses, complementing the feel of the village. Although the course has been altered and toughened slightly over the years, the original charm remains.

A picturesque view from the elevated 1st tee gets the round off to a pleasant start. The tree-lined fairway, climbing up toward a raised green, makes for an appealing target with 3-wood in hand. The green is protected by deep, creatively shaped bunkers, the first in a sequence of interesting sand traps. Another good view is rewarded from the 2nd tee, but this time it is of an intimidating carry over a gorge cutting diagonally through the hole. The longer the drive, the straighter the angle of the green for the approach, and at 466 yards/426 m many will be hitting a long club at a green angled away to the right.

An interesting feature at St. George's is that the fairways are rarely mowed in a straight line, instead bulging and narrowing to accentuate the holes. On the par-5 9th, for example, the fairway opens wide to accommodate shorter tee shots, while those looking to take too much distance from the tee will find the target is narrowed by two daunting bunkers pinching into the fairway from both sides. The same applies for the second shot, when a layup

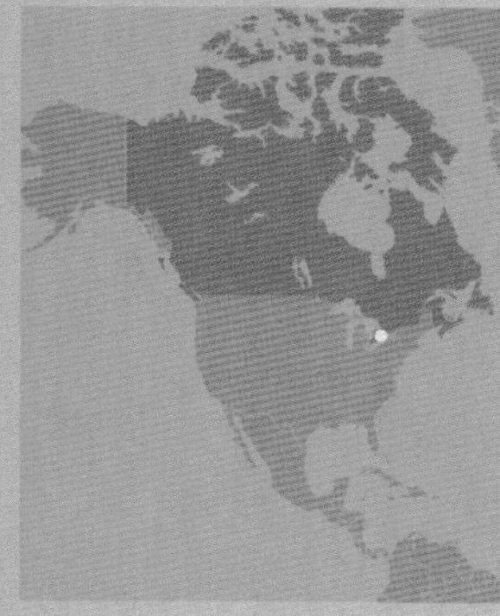

is played to a relatively large portion of short grass, but the fairway gets tighter toward the green, so one thinks twice about attempting to get on in two.

Tough finish

A formidable finishing stretch begins on the 14th, a long par 4 with a river in play down the right-hand side, which eventually cuts across the front of the green. Many players will have to play this as a three-shot hole rather than chance the river with a long iron. Holes 17 and 18 used to be par 5s, and the accommodating bulges of the fairways are similar to the set-up of the 9th. The difficulty is that, as they are now par 4s, one must take on the tighter, longer lines previously designed for someone trying to get on under regulation. Despite the tough finish, a feeling of relaxation prevails on the short walk to the traditional clubhouse, the gentle hills, weaving fairways, and tranquil river making St. George's a delightful course in true English style.

CARD OF THE COURSE

Hole	Distance (yards)	Par	Hole	Distance (yards)	Par
1	370	4	10	377	4
2	466	4	11	528	5
3	198	3	12	399	4
4	474	5	13	213	3
5	432	4	14	466	4
6	201	3	15	570	5
7	446	4	16	203	3
8	223	3	17	470	4
9	538	5	18	451	4
Out	3,348	35	In	3,677	36
			Total	**7,025**	**71**

▶ After U.S. golfer Art Wall had won the 1960 Canadian Open with a score of 19-under, Stanley Thompson's protégé and friend, Robbie Robinson, was brought in to toughen up the course. He remodeled five of the holes, including the 4th (pictured left).

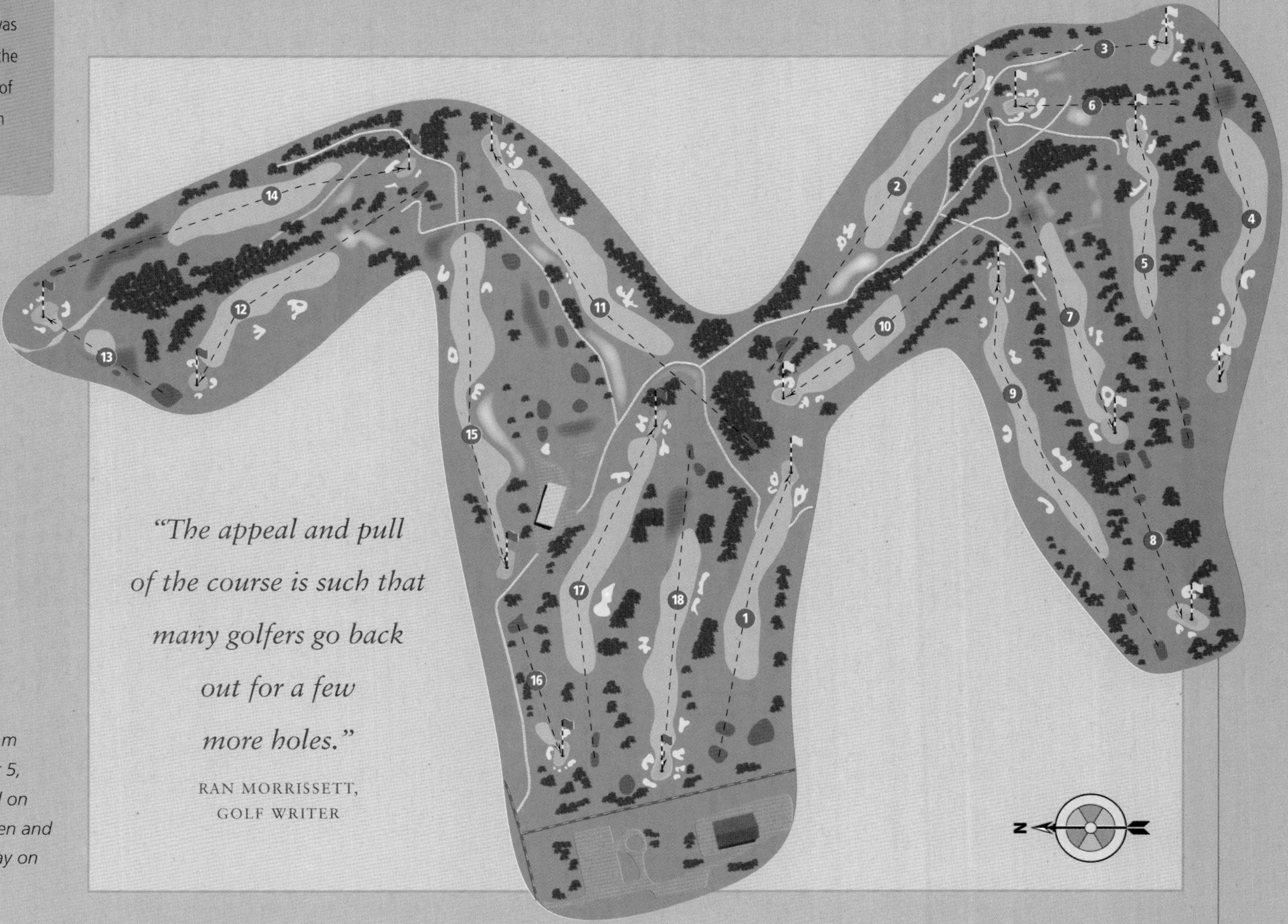

"The appeal and pull of the course is such that many golfers go back out for a few more holes."

RAN MORRISSETT, GOLF WRITER

LEFT *At 474 yards/433 m the 4th is short for a par 5, but it is tightly bunkered on the approach to the green and trees constrict the fairway on both sides.*

Courses 47–56

CARIBBEAN
47 Mid Ocean, Bermuda
48 Tryall, Jamaica
49 Casa de Campo, Dominican Republic
50 Mahogany Run, U.S. Virgin Islands

CENTRAL & SOUTH AMERICA
51 Cabo Del Sol, Mexico
52 Vista Vallarta, Mexico
53 Papagayo, Costa Rica
54 The Jockey Club, Argentina
55 Ilha de Comandatuba, Brazil
56 La Dehesa, Chile